Author contact krisfez@yahoo.co.uk

Stance books in association with East & West

www.eastandwest.me

CIM FEZ

LEGALISATION

RETHINKING DRUG POLICY

IN A GLOBALISED WORLD

STANCE BOOKS

IPSWICH, UK

ISBN 9798670686402

STAN

TO MY MUM

ROSEMARY FESSLER

CONTENTS

ABOUT THE AUTHOR

Cim Fez was born in Canada in 1976 and after leaving North America would spend the next decade between the UK and Switzerland the countries of his parents' birth. Most of his secondary education followed in the UK. He was awarded his bachelor's degree in modern languages from the University of Essex, where he would also conclude studies in the Modern History of Russia. In 2014 Cim would complete a masters in Transnational Crime in Cambridge at Anglia Ruskin.

He currently works for the NHS in a treatment and assessment unit for people with learning difficulties. Additionally, Cim has obtained many years of experience working for social services with people afflicted by drug addiction. This work gave him a first-hand account of the social problems that can arise from drug misuse, whether this be due to the dysfunctional lifestyles drug addiction invariably promotes or due to its associated brushes with the law. While working for social services it also became apparent how these socially maladjusted individuals at times manage to perpetuate cycles of dysfunction in further generations. This generally being associated with a mindset that is beholden or at the very least prioritises drugs over any other issue in their individual orientated worlds.

Supplementary to his career in the British social/ health sector Cim has volunteered overseas, working with refugees in a charity centre run by UNHCR in the Republic of Moldova, this work also included joint projects with other NGOs such as the International Office of Migration. This work allowed for a greater understanding of the psychological impact of conflict, but also provided an introduction to the global issues of people smuggling and human trafficking. In his role at the charity centre he not only helped look after the wellbeing of the refugees present but helped promote their plight by participating on projects to increase awareness of the issues at hand and by seeking to integrate the victims of war into the local communities.

Cim is a regular contributor for the news outlet East & West where he writes on Russia and the post-Soviet space, international relations, current affairs and international governmental organisations.

On a more personal level he enjoys participating in most sports and has a keen interest in languages. Cim has been teaching himself Chinese for over three years but admits frequently that he still can't pronounce a single sentence correctly. R Sattler

Introduction

In 2018 an article entitled "Opioid s of the Masses, Stopping an American Epidemic from Going Global" appeared in the May addition of Foreign Policy magazine. It was a piece that brought home the horrific truth of the drug crisis that is currently sweeping across North America and while the story in its entirety made uncomfortable reading, there were three particular facets of the story that must cause great disquiet not only for the US political class, but also for governments across the globe. The first point that astounds is on a statistical level. "From 2000 to 2016, more Americans died of overdoses than died in World War I and World War II combined" this horror is redoubled when we consider that the number currently living with addiction by far outweigh the referred to death toll. This realisation naturally promises an increased number of the latter. The second and perhaps most worrying aspect the story brings to light is the probability that this epidemic will advance across the world and finally the third disconcerting point appears to be the involvement of multinational corporations, that according to the authors have played a significant role in this wave of addiction as the ensuing quote from the text explains " Facing a backlash in the United States and Canada, drug companies are turning their attention to Asia and Europe and repeating the tactics that created the crisis in the first place. At the same time, the rise of fentanyl, a highly potent synthetic opioid has made the outbreak even deadlier and begun to reshape the global drug market. A development with significant foreign policy implications ". The Foreign Affairs piece suggests tackling the corporations who have been profiting from the sale of opioid s by introducing more punctilious regulation, removing the licence of unscrupulous doctors who abuse their role and by empowering law enforcement agencies to prosecute "gross corporate malfeasance", all of which seems entirely intuitive, however there are complications, the drug abusers will remain, therefore demand too will persist, leaving organised crime syndicates to fill the void. It is the perennial dilemma in the war on drugs, that where one issue is addressed a further problem arises elsewhere, analogous to the myth of Hydra where for every head chopped off another two are immediately regrown. It is the aim of this book no less to address these issues with the intention of seeking new solutions to what by now feels like an eternal problem. (Humphreys et al 2018)

We start by looking at Legislation which often serves as a form of social demarcation, informing society where a given states boundaries rest on all matter of spheres from taxation to crime, to citizenship. In relation to the drugs market the most significant piece of legislation introduced was the Harrison Narcotics Tax Act implemented in the United States on the 17th of December 1914 (Musto 1999). The Harrison Act forbade the recreational use and distribution of opiate and coca leaf based products. An exception for medical / therapeutic use and industrial production in line with licensing and tax registration was however catered for (Musto 1999)(Van Duyne 2005). In many respects the Acts proscription into law may be considered a watershed moment in the prohibition of psychoactive substances, not just within the confines of the United States where religious puritan moralism sought to crack down on all forms of vice, corruption and intemperance that had been gripping the nation since the late 19 hundreds (Musto 1999). Indeed the Harrison Act can justly claim to be the ground law upon which drug policy and therefore drug prohibition has been based worldwide for the past century (Stares 1996)(Van Duyne 2005).

Despite prohibitions longevity the criminalization of narcotics is often conspicuous by its hotly contested nature among policy makers and academics alike and provides another political realm in which the traditional foes, that is to say libertarians and conservatives collide. Conservatives often, although not exclusively are considered to be beholden to the current doctrine of prohibition (Hitchens 2012), while those often associated with a more liberal constitution envisage varying degrees of decriminalization or even full-blown legalization (Hitchens 2012).

Notwithstanding several recent developments in Switzerland, Holland, Mexico and Portugal where varying degrees of decriminalization have been introduced on a national level, the overwhelming response to drug distribution, consumption and production has been based on negative or punitive laws that are embodied in the dominant prohibitive policies (Chambliss et al 2010). However debates to the actual effectiveness of prohibition have been coming more and more to the fore in recent years, with many citing the drug war as "Ineffective "or even "lost" (Cardozo et al 2009)(Clegg & Branson 2015)(Townsend 2014). Furthermore, are the changing dynamics in the on-going processes of globalization not accentuating the need for a policy rethink? That is to say, are inadequate policies conceived of in an era defined by the nation state likely to prove efficient in a post-modern world where sovereignty encapsulated by rigid national boundaries' that once limited trade both licit and illicit appear to be withering away? (Naim 2005)

The amalgamation of states into regional bodies such as the EU, ASEAN, NAFTA or the Eurasian Union coupled to neoliberal policies has radically changed notions of the Westphalian state (McGrew 2011) and eased the distribution of merchandise, goods, capital and people in both a logistical and financial sense (Held et al 2000). Processes which have been meticulously exploited by both transnational organized crime (TOC) and international terrorism, constituting a security threat to states across the world (Naim 2005). Therefore, an examination of the legitimacy of prohibition as a policy in the globalised era will be an integral part of this work. We commence by presenting the historical background to prohibitions rise. Investigating its efficacy and the methods employed in the war on drugs. Thereafter we shall examine the role that globalization is playing within the development of the illicit drug market. We will then move on to Passas adaptation of Durkheim's anomie, which he applies in conjunction with globalization. In the final chapter I shall be addressing issues around global policing and presenting alternative policies, before finally attempting to make some recommendations based on the findings.

Chapter 1

Prohibition

The worldwide criminalization of narcotics has its roots in the puritan moralism of 19th century "nativist" America, which traditionally embraced the Calvinist protestant religious doctrines from whence the many temperance movements such as the Woman's Christian Temperance Union and Anti Saloon League were inspired (Abadinsky 2003). The aforementioned groups are typically associated with the prohibition of alcohol that came into force with the signing of the Volstead Act in 1919, however they are also synonymous with what was in effect a war on "vice" that seemed to be magnifying with the rapid urbanization and industrialization that was besetting America at the time. Van Duyne Professor of Empirical Penal Science at the University of Tilburg highlights a concern among certain pious sectors of society for what he refers to as the "right state of mind" which seemingly induced resolute devotees to "crusade against "bad habits" in general and bad substances in particular"(Van Duyne& Levi 2005) the preponderance of theological explanation in the condemnation of mind altering substances is accordingly documented by G Klerman who identified the eminence of pharmacological Calvinism not only within prohibitive circles, but in the drugs debate at large (Klerman 1972). Pharmacological Calvinist conjecture involves a "general distrust of drugs used for non-therapeutic purposes and a conviction that if a drug makes you feel good, it must be morally bad" as a consequence Klerman cites the relevance of "abstinence as the highest ideal"(Klerman) Notwithstanding the clear leverage that ecclesiastical deliberations played in developing prohibitive policies their rise as an orchestrated cause appears to be centred on the fear of culturally divulging "outer" groups or foreign migrants who had steadily been arriving on US shores to feed into the burgeoning industrialization that defined the era. (Van Duyne& Levi 2005)

The struggle for prohibition therefore became a proxy battle for societal hegemony between the old and the newer urban and overwhelmingly foreign communities that were beginning to take root. It was nothing more than the pitting of the traditional nativist and rural way of life against the city dwellers which now comprised a new wave of immigrant, whose ethnicity was generally of Germanic, Italian, Chinese or East European decent (Abadisnky 2003). These immigrants brought with them not only divulging cultures, but also linguistic and religious variations to the Anglo-Saxon pioneers who had preceded them (Abadinsky 2003). As a consequence Religion one may suggest was nothing more than a catalyst by which the inner group sought to reaffirm itself in the face of the ontological insecurities brought on by an era of accelerated change, both in the demographics of the nation and in the intensified means of production. Prohibition in sum can be viewed as a reactionary policy based on the primordial musings of intolerance and was directed at this "immoral invading foreign other" (Kleiman et al 2011).

This "foreign face" of narcotic consumption is embodied in the media messages of the time, messages which clearly sought to propagate fear. The slogan "Yellow peril" common at the time denotes the evil Chinese opium smoking "mongers" who would seduce young innocent white girls into a life of eternal vice (Van Duyne & Levi), while Marijuana and Cocaine were considered the profligacy of the Mexican labourer and the African American respectively, such omnipresent portrayals lead naturally to a consolidation of social insecurities and the introduction of punitive orientated policies (Kleiman et al).

The fact that criminalization was directed principally against a foreign and often "subhuman other" reduced control mechanisms that could have reigned in harsh punitive sanctions against legal infringements once drugs had been prohibited under federal law. This lack of restraint in seeking punishment for those we fear is however, consistent with inner group socio-psychological dynamics and is eloquently expressed in the work of Janis who's research led her to conclude that "Here members of the group become excessively protective of the group as an entity, restricting membership to those also loyal to the group, isolating themselves from any information counter to their own image of the group, and viewing threats to their policies as threats to the group. Because of the insular quality of such groups, they can take extreme actions without realizing the impact (Janis 1989). These conclusions are reaffirmed by Van Duyne who alludes to the traditional zero tolerance approach undertaken by US enforcement policies in relation to psychoactive substances. He points to their full prohibitive nature "buttressed by the force of law. No reduction by socialization of bad habits, but demonization and criminalization of wicked habits" (Van Duyne & Levi 2005).

That prohibition would be implemented on a global scale, has a lot do with the projection of events happening within North America at the time and the subsequent internationalization of US foreign policy. It has also been claimed that US prerogatives were born out of their failure to create a niche in the opium market that remained firmly in the grasp of the old colonial powers and by moves to improve their racist/anti-Chinese image that had arisen due to the maltreatment many Sino immigrants had experienced at the hands of their US patrons (Van Duyne and Levi 2005). As a result of these factors a series of conventions and treaties including the Hague treaty of 1912, the international opium convention of 1925 and the 1931 convention for limiting the manufacture and regulating the distribution of narcotic drugs were presented internationally at the behest of the US government (Musto 1999). These agreements have since been superseded by the three UN conventions on narcotics, the most recent of which is the 1988 UN convention against the illicit traffic in narcotic drugs and Psychotropic Substances (UNODC). These conventions provide the perfect infrastructure by which the US was able to internationalise its domestic drug policies with general acquiescence, despite some hesitation on the part of the traditional colonial powers before the second world war (Bewley Taylor 2001).

Chapter 2

The case for prohibition

In this chapter we shall be looking at the case for prohibition. Two principle arguments which form the basis for the criminalization of drugs have been identified.

I. That legalization would increase consumption leading to higher addiction rates
II. Higher addiction rates would lead to increased damage to health, both to society and the individual (MacCoun et al 1993)

These two arguments are then expanded upon, with advocates of criminalization fearing that legalization would lead to wholesale family disintegration and disproportionate harm to ethnic minorities who traditionally have been linked to drug misuse (23 Inciardi). Prohibitionists deduce that any policy change would give rise to increased levels of criminal activity, primarily due to the readily accepted "truism" that links pharmacological addiction to increased crime rates, as dependents seek deviant forms of financial accumulation in order to placate their intense cravings (Inciardi 1999). An additional argument put forward is that legalization/decriminalization would act as nothing more than an endorsement of psychoactive substances, perceptually minimizing the health risks incurred by taking drugs in the eyes of the public and hence leading to a diminution of social control mechanisms, the consequences of which would lead to a massive increase in drug consumption and therefore a public health catastrophe (Inciardi 1999). If such claims are just is hard to ascertain, but it certainly does appeal to common sense and there does appear at first glance to be a strong correlation between prohibition and a reduction in drug consumption. In 2009 the United Nations presented a 100 year analysis on the development of the global drug market in which Antonio Maria Costa executive director of the United Nations office on drugs and crime gave a glowing account of prohibitive policies which had seen opiate consumption fall from 25 million in 1906 to 16.5 million in 2006, statistics which equate to a reduction from 1.5% to a 0.25% use rate amongst the world population (UNDOC 2008). Since then misuse has risen to between 27.9 to 38 million users or approximately 0.6%- 0.8% of the global population (UNDOC 2015). What's more the statistic is obtained by the typological separation of opioids from opiates despite both deriving from the same *lachryma papaveris* base. By combining both categories use soars to between 40-58 million or between 0.9 -1.2 % of the world's population (UNDOC 2015). Factors such as US deaths due to heroin induced overdoses, which have doubled from 1779 in 2010 to 3661 in 2012 dampen Costas optimism yet further (Guardian 2014). Additionally there are important considerations that must be taken into account when comparing 1906 with 2006, one of which is the realization that an overwhelming majority of opiate users in 1906 were to be found in China, a figure put at 16 million by Newmann (Newman 1995) while other prominent markets such as those in Iran, Indonesia, Malaysia, Burma, Pakistan, Bangladesh and the Philippines defined the unequivocally Asian nature of consumption at the time, contrasting starkly with the situation today (Paoli et al 2009). As we see in the pie chart below, heroin use is now a global phenomenon (Jenner 2014). ***Source Handbook of Transnational Crime and Justice 2014. M S Jenner***

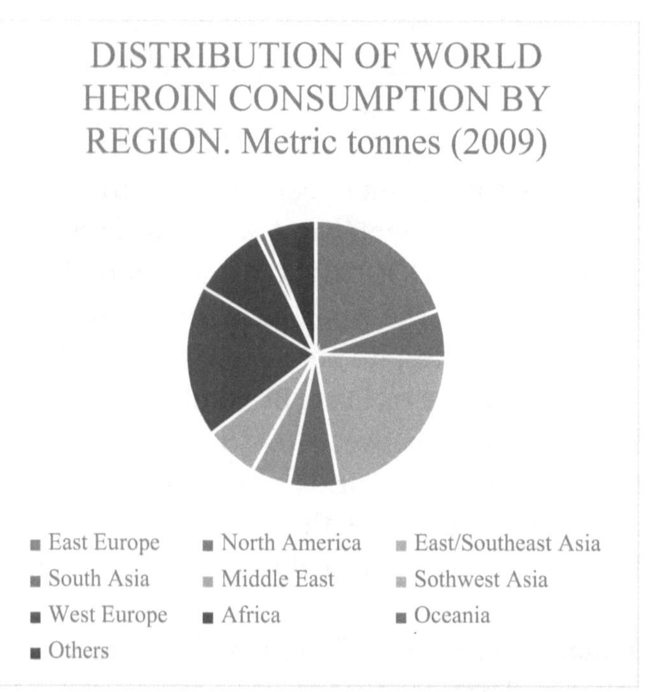

Also a very real difference in potency between the opiates available in 1909 and the heroin largely consumed today is apparent, as the following statement confirms "A whole generation of new historians believe that most users, including many regular users, were still able to lead normal lives and suffered no negative consequences from their opium use". (Newmann 1995) It is an account that echoes with Dikoetter who correspondingly notes that "In most cases habitual opium use did not have the significant harmful effects on either health or longevity" (Dikoetter 2004) and as such must be deemed significantly less hazardous than the heroin available around the globe today. As was seen during the period of alcohol prohibition in the United States 1919-1933 the criminalization of a substance invariably leads to that substance increasing in strength as people look to modify the weights of illicit produce not only to maximize profitability but also to reduce the risk of getting caught (Thornton 1991).

Moreover, the contemporary illicit drug market has diversified, with sellers providing a cornucopia of substances ranging from cannabis, cocaine, heroin, ecstasy, LSD, magic mushrooms, ketamine and an array of amphetamines amongst many others. It is a market of choice in which, according to the UN global drugs report of 2012 there were between 162 million and 335 million users, corresponding to between 3.5 and 7% of the world's population (UNODC 2015).

The cornerstone of prohibitionist policy are the zero tolerance attitudes applied to both drug dealers and drug abusers by criminal justice systems across the world. It is reasoned that tough sentencing to both those who demand and those who supply drugs will deter individuals from initiating drug consumption, but the harsh penalties that have led to 500000 US incarcerations on drugs offences (at the expense of the tax payer) at any one time (Kleiman et al 2011) or even the sterner measures employed in China, Iran, Saudi Arabia and Vietnam or a whole host of countries, where they sentence drug traffickers to death, has not managed to stifle the market (Count the costs 2012). If anything, criminalization has provided an opportunity for clandestine entrepreneurs to benefit from the creation of illicit markets. The prohibitive nature of which invariably ensures high recompense on the goods being sold (Count the costs 2012). Further criminalization has removed quality control policies on the products being produced. This has created an environment in which drug users can never be sure exactly what they are taking (Count the costs 2012), as highlighted by the three deaths in Ipswich over the festive period 2014, a case in which the users believed they were taking MDMA, instead the pills after analysis turned out to contain PMMA (Adams 2015). In addition, the purity of most drugs smuggled are reduced by the repeated "cutting" of the product which provides enhanced profitability. The properties with which drugs are bulked are often cited as being sinister and deleterious to consumer's health. Prohibition itself is also charged with failing to prevent disease, in that it deprives users' access to harm reduction programmes that provide safe injection rooms, where addicts may obtain counselling, clean syringes and medical attention (Count the costs 2012). Leading even some adherents of prohibition to call for a change, nevertheless harm reduction is still seen to contravene international policy as the UNs International Narcotic Control Board reaffirmed.

"The board believes that any national, state or local authority that permits the establishment and operation of drug injection rooms or any outlet to facilitate the abuse of drugs(by injection or any other route of administration) also facilitates illicit drug trafficking...By permitting drug injection rooms, a Government could be considered to be in contravention of the international drug control treaties by facilitating in, aiding and/or abetting the commission of crimes involving illegal drug possession and use, as well as other criminal offenses, including drug trafficking"

(Chambliss et al 2010)

Chapter 3

Prohibition of alcohol lessons from the past

Philosophically speaking the safeguarding of public health through prohibitionist policies is complicated by the apparent contradiction that is the legalization of tobacco and alcohol, substances associated with grave health consequences. According to the world health organization 5.4 million people die a year due to smoking (WHO 2015) while in 2012 alcohol accounted for 3.3 million deaths (WHO 2015), this compares with 95,000-231,400 worldwide drug related deaths. (UNODC 2015) Such contradistinctive results however provide no certain basis for the legalization of drugs and provide no concrete evidence to suggest what's available on the black market is safer than either tobacco or alcohol; it does however challenge the political authority that promotes criminalization on the grounds of health. Moreover for those who support criminalization, it is the availability of both tobacco and alcohol that is the contributing factor in the 8.7 million deaths mentioned previously, therefore we must be thankful that well known addictive substances such as crack cocaine and heroin are banned, as it is their restricted availability that protects us from a drug epidemic (Inciardi 1999) (Kleiman et al 2012), but such a view equally appears to be nothing more than conjecture.

Alcohol and narcotics are not comparable variables. Alcohol especially has been culturally embedded in many parts of the world, having been discovered by Europeans presumably during the Neolithic period (Clark 1976), it is also conspicuous by its use in religious rituals and ceremony (Behr 1997). At no time has drug consumption ever reached such proportions across the globe. (Paoli et al 2009)

Arguments pertaining to the US prohibition of alcohol have been cited by Clark as evidence that prohibition works and it certainly appeared successful upon implementation, but it became clear that year on year larger and larger quantities of drink were being ingested.

As we see from the annual per capita consumption in the table that follows (Thornton 1991).

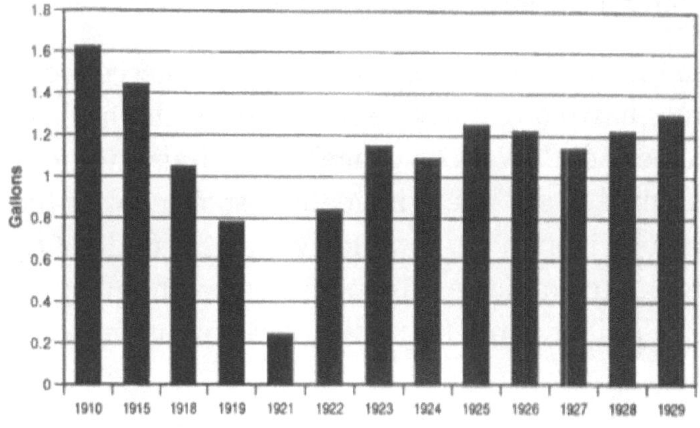

Interestingly the table above reveals a gradual decline in consumption leading up to the introduction of prohibition in 1919. This is attributed to the successful evangelical campaigns that portrayed alcohol as an evil. It reveals the power of socialization that could be used to combat drugs and confirms a process that helped reduce alcohol use from 32 L in 1810 to 9.5 L in 1850 (Clark 1976).

What eventually helped lead to prohibition being repealed was however was the rise of organized crime and the violence it brought to the streets of America (Thornton 1991). Hence a discrepancy in policy is apparent and begs a pertinent question. If the 100000 deaths related to drug crime in Mexico (Tuckman 2015) or the 220000 deaths that have accompanied Columbia's drug funded civil war (Guardian 2013) had taken place in the United States or Germany, would we have witnessed a policy shift by now?

Given the ineffectiveness of prohibition, successive regimes have sought to give the policy teeth, this has led to periodic " Wars on drugs" these dramaturgically proclaimed "wars" are principally associated with the efforts of Nixon in 1971 and Reagan in the mid-1980s. Their aim to eradicate this "public enemy number one". (Vulliamy2011) (Guardian archives online)

Chapter 4

The "war on drugs"

The war on drugs is nothing more than an extension of prohibition. Its aims are to reduce if not completely nullify the existence of the illegal drugs market and it includes a package consisting of military aid and military interventions in source countries. It was hoped that together with a zero-tolerance stance towards narcotics in the domestic sphere, that this now proverbial "war on drugs" could stem the flow of supply or at least render it insignificant (McCoy 1972). The policy so far has been unable to meet expectations. The quixotic "war on drugs" has employed both negative and positive control strategies as a means to fulfil its objective. Negative control measures are identifiable as those provisions which rest upon the use of coercive tactics or the threat of sanctions, i.e. lengthy prison sentences, while positive measures promote rewards for abstinence etc (Stares 1996). Kleiman et al have identified three key strategies which have been deployed in the war on drugs they concentrate predominantly on the disruption of supply, they are alternative development, eradication and interdiction (Kleiman et al 2011). These strategies while developed with the best of intentions have more often than not only increased drug production, as such it comes as no surprise that the World Drugs Report of 2018 concluded that the figures for the years opium production were "easily the highest estimate recorded by the UN Office on Drugs and Crime since monitoring started at the beginning of the twenty first century". For Cocaine manufacture the situation is similar with the highest levels of production ever being recorded in 2016 (UNODC 2018). In the following sections we examine exactly how this situation has come to pass, but first we must acknowledge a significant paradox that rests at the heart of the war on drugs, then it is prohibition itself from which narcotics derives its high rates of profitability, hence the international communities efforts to establish effective alternative development arrangements (by encouraging farmers to grow sugar or coffee instead of heroin) are undermined due to the drugs greater profit margin, a profit margin obtained as a direct consequence of its illegal status. With this in mind we turn our attention to the "positive" concept of alternative development in order to assess its efficacy.

Alternative development

Alternative development (AD) is the practice whereby crop growers of opium, coca or marijuana are encouraged to harvest legal produce instead of narcotics; examples include avocados in Michoacán (Flannery 2014), a heroin producing region of Mexico or vegetables, fruits and nuts in Afghanistan (AECOM). Subsidies are provided to increase the profitability for those who seek to grow alternatives. The principal unfortunately has been beset by troubles, despite the good intentions behind the scheme. One significant issue is directly related to development and concerns the poor infrastructure that exists in drug producing hotspots. A lack of highways, suitable roads, transport links etc, invariably means that by the time fresh produce can be transported the vegetables etc are often spoilt (Stares 1996)(Keefer&Loayza2010). Further complications also arise from the price of transportation. These two realities mean produce may not only be of poorer quality but also too expensive to compete with already established competitors in faraway places (Stares 1996).

Additionally, instability and insecure environments such as those found in Afghanistan, Columbia, Mexico etc. cannot guarantee the farmers a livelihood, especially in respect of the time needed to reap the benefits of the new crops. Moreover, areas controlled by guerrilla groups are out of bounds to such approaches, they lie beyond the control of central governments (Stares 1996) and where farmers have been approached criminal and terrorist groups can simply outbid the incentives being presented to cultivators. Farmers have also been known to resort to growing legal and illicit produce synchronously, hence reaping the benefits that come with state subsidies while maintaining profits from narco production (Kleiman et a 2011).

Indeed, the policy can be viewed as ipso facto dangerous, as it may create what is known as the balloon effect, as drug gangs simply seek alternative areas of production, cultivation etc (Jenner 2014). Therefore, one is aiding the dissemination of the drugs problem. Drug trafficking routes and zones of production being well established as a causatum for addiction in local communities, not only are crop producing regions more numerous, but so too is demand (Keefer & Loayza 2010).

The above listed scenarios unfortunately are the rule not the exception and describe the typical dynamics prevalent in countries like Afghanistan, Mexico or Colombia today. Despite some of the inherent problems identified above in relation to the strategy of alternative development, there are more substantial social, economic and political realities that leave AD programmes looking extremely naive. Then the international institutions seldom seem to factor in the patron-client relationships which ensure the harvesting of coca or opium based produce. It must be recognised that whole sectors of the economy have become reliant on its income, meaning the farmer at source is not simply an isolated individual, rather a node in a complex network of often very powerful interests. The business associated with the crop, hence is a driver for local markets, employment and the economy overall. It may influence local developments in ways unseen to international enforcement agencies.

As Gutierrez found in his research on the subject *"the illicit commerce is of a magnitude likely to leave almost no aspect of development untouched. Like sugar and coffee, its sheer size and scope will shape access to land and markets; affect the creation of employment; sway trends in banking; and drive cross-border financial flows. It will also likely affect public services; influence political decision-making; and change processes on who gets to wield power, among others. In other words, the impact and consequences – intended and unintended – are significant"* (Gutierrez 2020). Little wonder that AD by and large has not managed to stem the flow of either opium or coca related products from source nations. Although it seems counter intuitive, we must recognise that drug cultivation in certain regions of the world is inextricably linked not only to the livelihoods of those who grow the crop, but that it in essence provides security too. The reliability and robust nature of the plants not to mention the business interlinked with the products ensure that drug production offers a sound survival strategy in countries beleaguered by conflict.

Alternative development schemes are often interlinked with eradication programmes as a two-pronged attack on drug manufacturing, but the latter too has often flattered to deceive.

Eradication

Eradication is perceived as a much more "negative" and punitive measure to disrupt the flow of drugs (Stares 1996). It is usually achieved by spraying fields from the air or by manual eradication, which entails enforcement officers digging up the fields where coca, marijuana or poppies have been planted (Keefer &

Loayza 2010). The down side to this, is that the farmers affected by the policy, who are generally extremely poor in the first place lose any kind of subsistence, hence forcing people into crime out of necessity, it may also facilitate recruitment to terrorist organizations in places such as Columbia and Afghanistan (Kleiman et al 2011). Alternatively, the farmers simply resort to planting twice as much of the crop in multiple locations as an insurance policy. As for using the planes to spray fields, well this is problematic in that it is damaging to the environment, hence its application has been banned in Bolivia and Peru but it's not just the chemicals which are damaging, farmers end up cutting down parts of the rain forest in order to grow and hide their crops amongst the dense jungles (Kleiman et al 2011) . Today and as a direct result of such policies, it is estimated that every gram of cocaine is responsible for 4 meters of Amazonian rain forest being destroyed (Nutt 2012). Analogous to alternative development it is worth remembering that any success in crop eradication may over time result in a ballooning effect, that is, causing the spread of the drugs industry elsewhere. There have been some notable examples of this ballooning effect where seemingly successful eradication programmes, have simply resulted in the relocation of production (Jenner 2014).

The table below shows how global cocaine production was unaffected by the Eradication programmes employed within Colombia during 1999. *See next page*

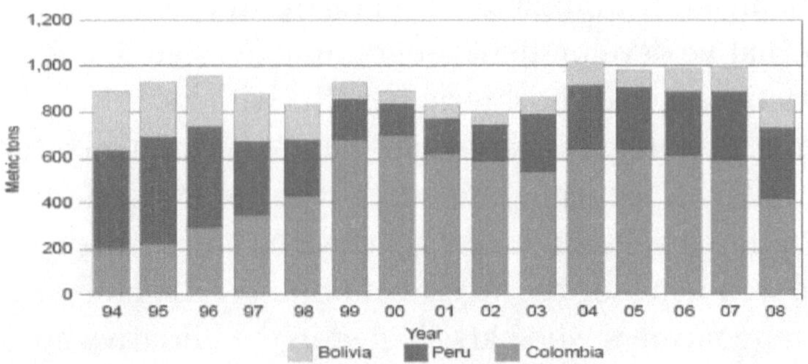

Figure 4: Global cocaine production (metric tonnes), 1994-2008 (UK Parliament)

The communities in drug manufacturing regions are highly resourceful and adept at facing challenges to their way of life, after all the cultivation of drug producing crops is often based on survival strategies. So, it is worth remembering that not all drugs are derived from plants, so eradication can and has at times lead to multifaceted drug production, as is becoming apparent in the Michoacán region of Mexico from where cocaine, heroin, marijuana and ATS are being trafficked (Tuckman 2015).

A prime example of the problems facing eradication were highlighted by Gutierrez in his study for the Routledge Research Group where he succinctly describes how an eradication program carried out in the Afghan region of Helmond by the British and US forces did more harm than good, despite initially appearing to be effective (Guiterrez 2020). Under the heading the "Food Zone Initiative" the governments of the two respective nations invested up to $18 million to reduce opium production, by offering cash in exchange for compliance to an eradication and alternative development programme. As stated, the initiative reaped short term benefits with local farmers earning higher incomes and developing better overall food security. This success however interfered with the social structures that ensured employment and wellbeing for the larger community. The land owning farmers who participated in the initiative no longer needed the farmhands or sharecroppers to toil their lands, the small holdings they rented out to seasonal migrant workers suddenly became unavailable. Three sectors of the local economy were suddenly excluded from the workforce and since only the land owners were able to access the programme they were denied any form of income. As a consequence, these groups were forced to migrate to other regions of the country, many settled just North of the Boghra canal beyond the reach of the US and UK funded schemes. The migrants would buy land from local commanders or work on already established farms. Often these migrants took credit from the locals with which they bought land. The newcomers helped transform 30,000 hectares of desert into agricultural and opium producing land. It is a scenario reminiscent of the enclosures that forced the British peasants off the land and into the factories at the start of the industrial revolution. In Afghanistan however there were no factories and the migrant workers invariably turned to what they know best. As a result, the region saw a 45-fold increase in opium cultivation, going from 752 hectares in 2002 to 37.270 by 2012 (Mansfield & Fishstein 2015).

Interdiction

The aims of interdiction are to intercept the transhipment of drugs, before they reach their destined markets (Jenner 2014). There have been notable success stories

especially concerning the seizures of cocaine, but despite these accomplishments deduction rates fall generally far below the 70% mark, which is adjudged to have an impact on supply. The nature of the drug market is also innately complex, given the fact that many substances are addictive, this provides for a certain inelasticity. So even obtaining 70% or above interdiction rates may not bring the required results

(Jenner 2014), criminal gangs would undoubtedly

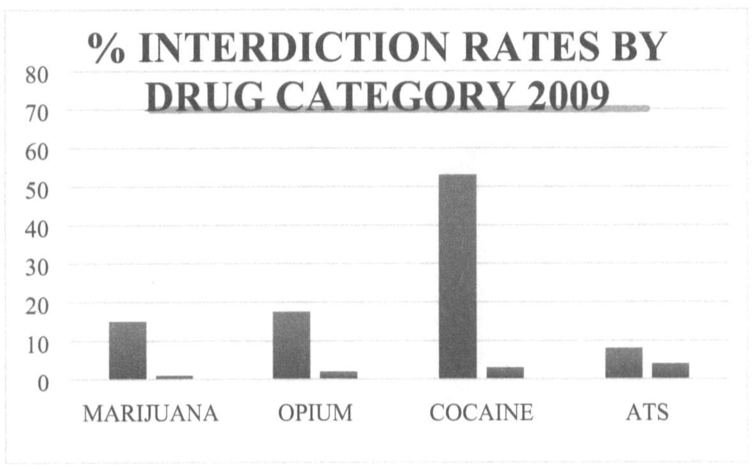

raise the price to compensate for the loss of profit. If price hikes effect consumption, is uncertain. It could elevate street crime as drug addicts seek means to placate their urges. Traffickers almost certainly would not lose their income (Jenner 2014). Smuggling networks are also extremely flexible and as such it is implausible bar a sudden technological breakthrough, ceteris paribus that a triumphal blow may be struck against the profiteers of prohibition (Stares 1996). *Table 2 interdiction rates by drug category. Green line indicates margin for success.*

Chapter 5

Globalisation

Globalization is playing an increasingly significant role in the drug debate (United Nations 1998). It is therefore essential to conduct a brief account of this worldwide process in order to understand exactly the transnational relevance of our metamorphosing world. Academics in the fields of the social sciences and economics confer that the modern epoch is one characterised by the rapid augmentation of transnational flows, above all the flows of trade, finance, human migration, information and the enmeshing of human civilizations not to mention the withering away of the state. These are all phenomena subsumed under the term "globalization" (Held et al 2000). Indeed, no other word is more apt at defining the worldwide dynamics that reflect the current zeitgeist. However social scientists have also observed the increasingly discernible dark side of globalization with such alarm that some have even suggested that the development of illicit flows and activities that have accompanied this process represents its real nature (Naim 2007) and it is these materialisations that are relevant to criminologists with regards to the drug markets. Paul B Stares succinctly explains how these global transformations have aided the growth of drugs markets.

"A world that is becoming increasingly "borderless," in which non-governmental or "transnational" actors play an ever-growing role in shaping the social, political, and economic life of the planet. The drug trade, as a consequence, has increasingly become a transnational phenomenon, driven and fashioned in critical ways by transnational forces and transnational actors." (Stares 1996)

There are however sceptics who repudiate globalization and see in transnational crime nothing more than the ancient art of smuggling. (Naim 2006) In their eyes the concept and indeed rise of the war on drugs is a conspiracy. A conspiracy structured on the careful manipulation of fear that is engineered in order to serve the hegemonic interests of US foreign policy and promotes their agenda for global governance (Sheptycki 2003). As Woodwiss posits "Drug trafficking is only one of several illegal activities that transcend national boundaries, but the American war on drugs has provided the crucial impetuses for a host of actions and agreements that otherwise would not have occurred (Woodwiss 2003).

The sceptical stance nonetheless is one that divulges from mainstream perceptions in relation to a corollary between the processes of globalization and the ascendency of narco-traffickers. For Naim the sceptics have failed to consider the changes that have taken place both politically and economically, nor have they contemplated the influence that revolutionary technologies have had in the hands of civilians or that the sealants " that governments traditionally relied on to secure their boarder have dissolved. Additionally, he cites the role of neoliberal economic reforms which have encouraged incentives to breakthrough these sealants legally or otherwise (Naim 2006). Ian Taylor in "Crime, Market Liberalism and the European Idea" gives an account of mainstream consensus by eluding to the distinct illations born of globalization and the simultaneous ascendency of the transnational drug trade, as he summarily notes "market liberal rhetoric recognises the transnational character of a selection of crime problems discussed in the public sphere specifically, transnational criminal trades in drugs and other substances "(Taylor 1998).

Taylor is far from alone in his analysis and his ideas are reflected by Toby Seddon in his work *"Drugs the informal economy and globalization"* where he elucidates on the four specific "realms" which the transnational drugs trade has managed to exploit in the ongoing processes of globalization. These four realms include trade, finance, migration and culture. (Seddon 2008) These we will now look at in greater depth.

Trade

Seddon in his work succinctly conveys how traffickers have exploited the trade links that expanded rapidly since the late 70s. Increased interconnectedness brought about by the deregulation of the market economy has enabled, both products and the transportation of goods from all across the world to enter new markets. Seddon cites the important role improved transport and communication networks have played in facilitating this transnational trade and how these legitimate factors have come to be exploited by those seeking to feed into the informal market. He illustrates the changing face of heroin consumption in the UK at the start of the 1980s as an example thereof (Seddon 2008). A period which saw a massive upsurge in recorded heroin addicts from 1000 at the start of the 1970s to a staggering 350000 by the end of the 1990s (BBC 2014). Van Duyne in "Drugs and Money" presents similar finding s across Europe at the start of the 1980s, indicating that the UK was not an isolated case. For Van Duyne heroin was a problem relatively isolated to North America, hence heroin addiction being referred to as the "American Disease" Europe traditionally was marked by a comparable absence of the drug (Van Duyne 2006). That a European surge in heroin abuse should coincide with the gradual removal of internal customs controls in what was formally known as the European Economic Community can barely be considered coincidental, indeed consistent increases between 1985, 2000 and 2017 are apparent when examining data on three fronts, firstly by noting significant increases in drug seizures for Heroin, Cocaine and Cannabis, and secondly by ascertaining that prices have remained stable or gone down depending on the substance, while purity has often increased, variables therefore indicative not just of a flourishing consumer market, but also of the ineffectual impact seizures have had on supply. It is a point substantiated by the UN report of 2019 which presupposes that the global health burden linked to the illicit use of drugs had hitherto been underestimated, the report follows this up by making reference to the half a million lives lost annually to

drug misuse (Van Duyne 2006)

Drug Seizures EU kg	*1985*	*1995*	*2000*	*2017*
Cannabis	170000	790000	790000	782000
Cocaine	1500	21000	26000	140400
Heroin	2000	5700	8400	22900

The table shows how overall trends in the trade of drugs are increasing (Above).

What is more the EMCDDA report of 2019 identified 55 new substances that have entered into the European market which equally made no significant impact on either the quality or price of both Heroin and Cocaine.

Perhaps one of the most interesting analysis presented in the 2019 ECMDDA s report concerns specific substance residues found in wastewater, this research pinpointed an upwards trend in Cocaine and Amphetamine use, although reductions were identified in the category concerning Methamphetamine. Notwithstanding the positive results on the latter, the general thirty-year upwards trend is certainly cause for concern.

When one considers that it is now possible to travel from Lisbon in far western Europe to Vladivostok in far eastern Asia some 10,000 Km with only one controlled border we begin to understand the impact that neoliberal policies and globalization have had (BBC 2013)(Dreyer&Popescu 2014) . A more shocking reality is that with Tajikistan's entry into the Eurasian Union (Schottenfeld 2015) the world's largest heroin producer will be separated from Europe by only two controls one of which (The Tadjik-Afghan border) is virtually non-existent given its highly permeable nature, a consequence of the widespread corruption that has taken hold in the former Soviet republic (Paoli et al 2009). To underscore the transformations that have benefited the narco-traffickers one can look at the rise in mere transportation and container traffic that has accompanied this internationalization. In 1991 the top ten seaports in the world dealt with 33.6 million containers. That's 23.2 million more than in 1981 (Stares 1996). This increase however pales into insignificance when we consider that in 2012 through Shanghai alone 32.5 million containers were recorded. (shiptechnology.com) If we consider that only three percent of the 9 million containers that entered the USA alone in the same year were inspected, we gain a concise understanding of the ease with which illicit substances may traverse the planet. That it takes five agents roughly three hours to examine a single container rather defines the futility of the task facing both border control agencies and states alike (Stares 1996).

Finance

There are various estimates ranging on the exact size of the transnational drug market, given the idiosyncratic informality of any illicit market precision is notoriously absent, even well-known specialists in the field quote substantially divulging figures. An evaluation by Robert J Kelly, professor emeritus in the Department of Criminal Justice and the Department of Sociology at Brooklyn College, New York, for example gives the illegal psychoactive drug market a value of $500 billion dollars a year (Kelly 2005), while the extremely influential Moises Naim editor of foreign policy and a former executive director of the World Bank deduces a number closer in the region of one trillion US dollars (Naim 2006). Despite the wide and incredibly varied range in their calculations it is apparent that we are dealing with extremely vast sums of money. Naturally an international market of such magnitude requires the existence of highly developed financial mechanisms which can expedite the transfer and exchange of money globally. Further due to the dangers inherent in the paper money trail left behind, those operating in any informal marketplace need a capacity for laundering money (Seddon 2008). These requirements have mostly been satisfied thanks to the liberalisation of financial controls in both the domestic and international setting but also due to the technological breakthroughs in communications and computing systems that have enabled real time financial transactions, 24 hours a day, right across the world to take place (Held 2008).

These processes of globalization, particularly the liberalization of the transnational financial system have all provided the perfect arena in which traffickers are able to launder their money and allow the enmeshing of both legitimate and illicit sources of income (Levi 2002). The legal void created by the delocalization of financial operations has created an environment in which national law enforcement has lost its territorial grounding. This loss is reflected in the rise of uncertainties among the policing community in regard to tackling the issue of money laundering. Both these insecurities and questions of jurisdiction have needless to say been extremely beneficial for criminal syndicates (Redo & Platzer 2014), Other issues of note that have proved conducive for the laundering of drug monies are systemic structural and personal related dynamics that accompanied the deregulation of the banking system. These include sub-cultures prevalent within financial organizations and the pressures placed upon their employees to maximise profits and out strip competition. This emphasis on goal driven policies added to weak regulation has often been equated with a fertile breeding ground for criminal activity in the corporate sphere. Much in keeping with classical criminological theories. (Tombs 2009) Indeed the pressure placed on staff to obtain high profits may lead to oversights or the weak enforcement of regulation which enables money to be laundered even in the absence of mens rea. In other words, the pressure to achieve results, can led to a negligence of duty which in turn allows for the laundering of money (Tombs 2009).

Advancements over the last thirty years in the international financial sector have been so crucial to the laundering of narco-dollars that it has allowed for the drastic augmentation of the illicit psychoactive market. As Seddon argues "The globalization of finance has underpinned the expansion of the global drug trade in recent decades, particularly through the increased capacity of the system to sustain large scale money laundering" (Seddon 2008).

Migration

In 2004 statistics put international migration at a conservative 175 million, to which a further 20 million refugees can be added, these figures highlight the explosion of human flows of migration taking place over the last two decades (Naim 2006). These flows have aided the development of transnational networks that at times have been and are being used for the transhipment of illicit drugs. These networks are primarily loose social and highly fluid structures that in their entirety form to create gangs or groups that come under the definition of organized crime (Seddon 2008) (Klerks 2003). These organizations coordinate their operations along logistical pathways that have evolved thanks to the current global changes (Klerks

2003). Often although by no means exclusively, such organizations may be constructed along ethnically homogenous lines. Examples include both Turkish and Kurdish gangs that have imported and distributed heroin to three major markets in the EU namely to the Netherlands, Germany and the UK (Van Duyne & Levi 2006). That ethnic criminal gangs are formed is often related to complex social issues such as a lack of assimilation in their new homelands but also to economic expectations not being fulfilled (Brown & Bean 2006). Therefore, the impact of *Differential opportunity* is not to be disesteemed. Immigrants often arrive in the West with unrealistic assumptions of what awaits them, the images of wealth and abundance conveyed via satellite TV and the internet contrast starkly with their newfound realities. Migrants often find themselves living in what Burgess defines as a zone of "*transition* "a term coined by his socio-biological interpretation of 1920s Chicago life, a city that gives this eponymous theory its name. The zone of transition is one synonymous with high rates of immigration, poverty, disease and crime (Hayward & Morrison 2009) further it is a zone of relative deprivation in which social strains are exacerbated by unfulfilled expectancies and as a result are promotive of crime. The Chicago School theory is clearly relevant today, with contemporary cities replicating the sociological pathologies that arose in an increasingly urbanized America at the start of the 20th century (Abdinsky 2003) In the modern era second generation Gastarbeiter may inadvertently transmit feelings of societal ostentation to newer immigrant communities and as such come to represent the embodiment of a subculture to whom the doors of legitimate success are barred (Brown&Bean 2006). With respect to these dynamics Ohnelin and Cloward list three distinctive categories within their theory of differential opportunity that can affect an individual's social control mechanisms and induce deviant behaviour, they are as follows.

1) *Retreatist subculture*: Here the individual exposed to social strains rejects normative goals such as wealth accumulation in favour of more obtainable goals, such as the "high "associated with drug consumption

2) *Conflict subculture*: In the conflict subculture social strains lead an individual to favour the use of violence and gang association to achieve status, again rejecting the norms emphasised by society

3) *Criminal subculture*: The criminal subculture as its name implies leads gangs to form cohesive structures that are perceived as organized crime. (Cloward&Ohlin 1960)

Key to these subcultures however is as the name infers "opportunity" As is true of legitimate means so is it true of the underworld. Opportunity is not equally distributed (Abadinsky 2003), but for migrants from certain corners of the world the links to their homelands gives access to illegitimate means. As Patel and Pearson observed in the West Yorkshire city of Bradford. They examined how immigrant Pakistani communities used their connections back home to shape "a complex unfolding of the relationship between drugs and the informal community" Pakistan at the time being notoriously accredited with a strong presence in the heroin trade. (Pearson & Patel 1998)

This brief analysis is by no means to be understood as an attack on migrant communities but is used as a concise tool to examine how the effects of globalization have impacted on the drug market. Not merely by providing ethnic homogenous pathways from source countries, but also due to social issues such as a lack of assimilation and strains brought about by relative deprivation.

Culture

For many the international developments taking place are not solely shaping flows of trade, finance, migration and information, but also merging cultures in a process that has come to be identified as Disneyization, or Americanization (Aas 2007), nouns that essentially underscore the pervasive nature of American culture that is being transmitted via satellite TV, music videos and the internet as well as via the ubiquitous consumerism associated with neo liberal driven capitalism. Nothing highlights the diffusion of the Americanization of youth culture more than the internationalization of rap music, a genre that has its origins in the black street ghetto life of the south Bronx, New York City. This form of music and its accompanying fashions have been embraced, seemingly by all corners of the globe (Aas 2007).

Worryingly for many observers is a definite glorification of violence, money and drug consumption that is prevalent in the hip hop genre. In a study conducted by Matt Daniels over 19000 Hip hop records mentioned forms of cocaine and Cannabis (Daily Mail2015)The ascendency not only of hip hop but more importantly of the internet and Satellite TV has led to a time and space compression across our planets. What once were faraway places can be reached with the click of a button, modern means of communications also provide for, the fluid conveyance of cultures, with youth now more than previous generations being overwhelmed by a myriad of belongings and identities. As Appanduauri points out, modern life is lived in various transnational scapes, etnoscapes, technoscapes, mediascapes, finacescapes and ideoscapes all of which impinge on an individual's identity and may transform cultural belonging in some part (Aas 2007). These processes one can surmise as the deterritorialization of culture (Aas 2007), which has been added to by an emphasis on consumerism, much to the detriment of many communities especially in areas of relative deprivation. These zones are unable to provide the environments conducive to delivering this sought-after consumer lifestyle by legitimate means. As a consequence, illegitimate means are promoted as the sole viable route to fulfilling the goals correlated to success (Aas 2007). This cultural shift to consumerism and the limited pathways by which to achieve this end are affirmed in the conclusions presented to us by the theory of differential opportunity as mentioned above.

As a result participating in informal economic activities such as the drug business allows those willing to take the risk a means to escaping poverty and more essentially a means to providing the much sought after consumer lifestyle. As Seddon infers "The global flow of consumer brands and symbols, from Nike trainers to Gucci watches, adds to the pressures in deprived localities to become involved in the informal economy and, consequently, in many cases with illegal drugs" (Seddon 1998) Seddon hence is making an assertion that corresponds to a breakdown of social controls in certain areas of our global community brought about by the strains of relative deprivation, it is a theme central to Mertons adaptation on Durkheims theory of anomie and as we shall see in the next section central to Passas theory of global anomie. *(On Accompanying disk please find a selection of videos that highlight changing global reference points and the role that media platforms play)*

Chapter 6

Global Anomie

In the previous section we examined Cloward and Ohlins theory of *differential opportunity* against a background of culture and immigration. We noted how these specific factors could play a decisive role in the advancement of the drug business. Their theory offers us a ratiocination for the development of both a retreatist and a criminal mind set within sectors of society. Naturally these factors can expound the drug problem by creating both a user (pull/demand factor) and drug entrepreneur (Push/supply factor). Central to their thesis however is the work of Emile Durkheim. It is his concept of *anomie* which lays the foundations for understanding the criminogenic moral breakdowns that may affect large sections of society placed under what Merton in the 1930s would identify as strain (Hayward & Morrison 2009). Durkheim's base theory is explicit in highlighting the criminogenic dyadic components intrinsic to capitalism, namely:

1) The promotion of self-interest

2) The inequalities in the division of labour. (Hayward &Morrison 2009)

According to Durkheim these factors combine to provoke feelings of estrangement and resentment in those veritably denied access to upward social mobility, hence offsetting deviance (Hayward & Morrison 2009). It is Merton who develops this functionalist paradigm still further by, as Hayward and Morrison have observed, calling attention to the *"gap between the ideal of a truly meritocratic society and the arbitrary realities of ones determining position within the social structure (Hayward & Morrison 2009).* Merton termed the stresses and sociological pressures born out of these inconsistencies and the inequivalence present in our communities as *strain (Hayward & Morrison 2009).* He also notes how education, media and marketing contribute to these sentiments. As Hayward and Morrison expand in their analysis of Merton's rubric *"Ironically the rise of literacy and the onset of institutions of universal education serves to make the situation worse, making promises about opportunities that the society is not able to deliver."* Before complimenting their perlustration by adding the role that mass cultural message distributed via advertisements etc. play in developing societal tensions (Hayward& Morrison 2009). More recently both Merton's and Durkheim's theories have been adapted to fit into the contemporary globalised world by the work of Nikos Passas, associate professor in criminal Justice at Temple University Philadelphia. In his paper on Global Anomie Passas reflects on the influence that satellite TV, the internet and the mass media in general have had in leading to a worldwide form of anomie. For Passas the images conveyed via these mediums have disseminated the dominant western cultural goals with its stipulation upon economic and materialistic advancement as well as a penchant for individualism, while simultaneously articulating the massive global stratifications that have intensified as an unintended result of neoliberal economic policies. Therefore, in accordance with Merton an "Overemphasis on success goals at the expense of normative behaviour" is apparent (Passas 2000). For Passas deviance is now provoked by transnational interactions that underscore the imbalanced nature of the world in which we live. These imbalanced interactions he concludes, provoke criminogenic asymmetries (Passas 2000).

Chapter 7

Investigating global anomie: Case study post-communist Russia

Passas research in relation to this theme concern post-communist Russia of the 1990s, which provides an appropriate litmus test. The drawing of the iron curtain opened the Russian audience to western film and media before the internet helped disseminate images of Western opulence, to those struggling to survive in a post-communist dystopia. The comparatively exuberant western way of life depicted in the imagery of Hollywood and MTV compounded by an increase in luxury consumer goods unobtainable to the general public expounded the strain experienced by many Russians.(Passas 2000) indeed that small minority of "new Russians" endowed with the means (often of ill-gotten gains) (Glenny 2008) to purchase such opulence exacerbated this strain still further while simultaneously heralding in a new domestic normative reference point, that seemed to confirm external ones (Passas 2000). Reference points that combine in their doctrines to shun the "socially important goals" associated with the old Soviet regime. (Pridmore & Kim 2006)(Passas2000)

This seismic cultural shift from socialism to consumerism however readjusted social goals beyond the means of the population at large. A research paper published in 1995 by Kuznetsova highlighted the sudden polarization of incomes, pronouncing a 28-fold difference between the top and bottom 10% (Kuznetsova 1995). Passas citing this statistic draws attention to "a lack of means to achieve ones goals in life" coalesced by a noticeable moral decay of those in authority that served only to encourage acts of deviance amongst the general populace and led to what Passas refers to as a set of rationalizations such as "It is okay to steal from the state" or "Everyone is doing the same"(Passas 2000). An accepted nonchalance to criminal behaviour therefore compounded already prevalent social strains brought on by poverty. These factors created a highly criminogenic environment and the increasing establishment of organized crime groups as well as retreatist deviance in which people use intoxication to escape from social disorientation (Passas 2000). Concurring with Passas perception of anomie is a study by Dafflon, in which he chartered the estrangement and social disorientation experienced by Russian teenagers and their potential to adopt deviant behaviour such as drug abuse, alcoholism or political radicalism as coping mechanisms (Dafflon 2009). These appear also to have found verification when examining statistical evidence by which we can gauge drug abuse in the Russian Federation since the fall of communism. (Paoli et al 2002)

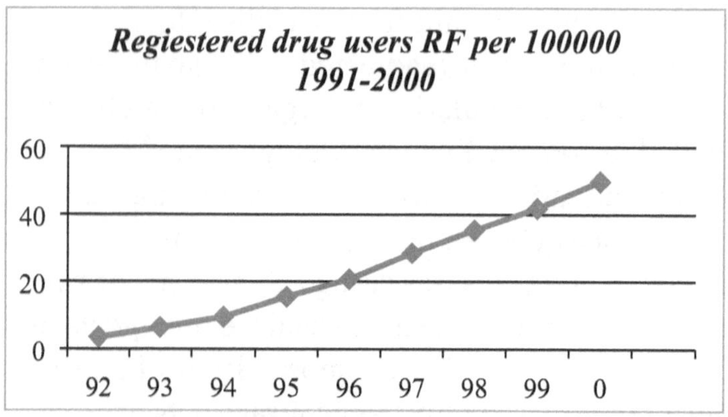

To reiterate, the data presented in the Russian case study are analogues with the anomic societal conditions that Durkheim identified in the years that followed the French revolution. The Russian case study interestingly provides both positive evidence of anomie in the years following the collapse of the Soviet Union, and a noticeable decline in the anomic state as Putinism helped deliver greater social stability, stability that above all has been predicated on traditional values, increasing living standards, a revival of religion and the return of Russian power on the global stage. The population at large have regained pride once more in their nation state, as a consequence Russians drink and consume less drugs than previously. There is nonetheless a caveat that must be considered, then the progress the Russian federation has undoubtedly made since 1991 is now under threat due to events in the Ukraine and the manner by which the West has ostracised Moscow from vast aspects of the global economy.

While all of the above focuses predominantly on the anomic conditioning of a developing Russian market economy. Passas nonetheless is definitive in analysing the role globalization has to play in the rise of crime. He refers to a form of global anomie spurned on by the predominance of neo-liberal policies that "foster new needs and desires that are all too often left unfulfilled" He comments on the "economic and power inequalities" that "have widened in and across countries in the last two decades" and the "enormous" populations that have "become more vulnerable to exploitation, criminal victimization and recruitment in illicit enterprises" (Passas 2000). Indeed, both the role of globalization as well as the development of failed states is cited by many observers as conducive to the illicit trade in psychoactive substances. Paul Stares concurs that the current internationalization of our world markets and culture will have severe negative repercussions and lead to a bifurcation of our world where the poor will have an even greater motivation to take drugs to increase productivity, dull hunger, relieve stress, or simply escape the harsh reality of the world they inhabit, before confirming the anomic conditions that are formed by conflict, failed and transitional states and their effects on drugs.(Stares 1996), The future therefore could be defined as ominous with " the incentives and opportunities to cultivate and manufacture drugs, transport them to the main centres of demand, and distribute them locally are already great and are only likely to grow in many areas of the world. Naim offers similar discourse in his book "Illicit" in which he replicates many of the ideas affirmed by Passas, linking globalization to new habits, new possibilities and endless opportunities for traffickers that are able to take advantage of those states that fall prey to political transformation or conflict (Naim 2006). The lawlessness subsumed in many a nation is also apparent to security operatives across the world, as is their ability to integrate into the global network. According to a CIA source there are now 50 regions around the world where governmental control is non-existent and where traffickers and terrorists have become the dominant political force (Naim 2006). That a nexus is now being established between *failed states-the drug business and terrorism* is firstly extremely worrying and secondly indicative of the failures inherent in current drug policy. A case study may be found in the former Soviet republic Tajikistan, which has perhaps become the consummate example of a failed state in which terrorism and the drug business have developed. Having gone through intense economic transformations, that is to say from a centrally planned economy to a capitalist marketplace. Tajikistan fell into a phase of anomie, from which a bloody civil war ensued. This in turn gave way to terrorist insurgencies (Paoli et al 2009). That today Tajikistan has developed into a narco-state is the affirmation of how rapidly things can go wrong. Tajikistan's role in the illicit drug trade is reflected in its rapid growth in Heroin seizures. In 1996 Tajik boarder security seized six and a half kilogrammes of Heroin, by 2002 this had increased to 4 tons with an estimated 80 tons passing through the territory undetected (Paoli et al 2009). These realities have shifted the drug debate into another dimension. Franko Katja Aas in her book crime and globalization is explicit in identifying both globalization and neo-liberalism as two key variables causative to the recent growth in the drug trade. She also notes the role the war on drugs has played in integrating policy in order to combat transnational organized criminal networks that are profiting from this illicit trade on a global scale (Aas 2007). Given that prohibition is the provocateur of an informal demand from which organized criminals and terrorists fund their operations in the early 21st century can we still claim that prohibition is a minimizer of risk rather than a precursor?

Chapter 8

Drug prohibition the political violence/ terrorism nexus

Criminologists in recent years as reflected in the work above, have come to view the processes of globalization as a facilitator to illicit markets of every genre (Aas 2007)(Baylis et al2011)(UNODC 2010). In addition, global anomie offset by deep inequality and cultural homogeneity not to mention new references points, has seen tensions rise in many regions of the world, particularly where more Western ideals and secularism have been pushing against conservative/ traditional or religious boundaries (Baylis et al 2011). That a fourth wave of democratization commenced in late 2010, known commonly as the Arab spring, is also often colloquialized as the Facebook revolution, epitomizes the era in which we currently find ourselves (Vargas 2012)(O'Donnell 2011). For some observers the importance of the Arab spring is found in its destabilizing qualities. The security dangers that have followed these uprisings have been egregious especially in Syria and Libya where terrorist organizations have sought to fill the power vacuum that followed the disintegration of authoritarian regimes (Hubbard, Worth & Gordon 2014). By scrutinizing these events, it is not unreasonable to conclude that globalization played its part in the dismantling and unfolding of a handful of these regimes (Hunter 2013) (Ghitis 2011). Ominously however is the way in which criminal elements have sought to take advantage thereof. It is not by coincidence that terrorism, much like illicit trade, has come to be known as the dark side of globalization (Powell 2002). For those working in security the Arab spring may be considered a sinister warning of future analogous occurrences to come, it is conceivable predominantly in regions where governments have a lax hand on control that uprisings , revolutions and insurgencies could occur as regimes fail to address the economic conditions that often beset weak nation states (Paoli et al 2011). What is clear is that economic interdependence and growing regionalism seems to have put paid for the moment to conflict among the world's most powerful nations (Hasenclever & Weiffen 2006)(Baylis et al 2011), however on the periphery of the global community we find no shortage of civil strife as governments struggle to deal with the ontological insecurities that afflict their citizens (Baylis et al 2011). For Martin Van Creveld modernity has been marked by exactly such a metamorphosis, he notes a specific change in the way war is now no longer fought between armies and states but has become replaced by terrorists and paramilitary organizations (Van Creveld 1991). Attacks such as 9/11 exemplify this approach as do the wars that have raged in Libya and Syria since 2010. Findlay concurs with this view and given the well-established nexus that exists between terrorist organizations and illicit markets is quick to suggest that state to state war has now been succeeded by crime as warfare (Findlay 2003). The nature of crime in conflict becomes evident when examining civil wars across the world since the end of the cold war, the development of crime among politically motivated organizations represents a shift in the way political insurgents have sought funding as state patronage ended with the fall of the iron curtain (Martin 2014)

This shift forced leftist/right wing guerrilla groups such as FARC and the AUC to adopt new means by which to conduct their operations. This invariably saw them enter the drugs trade. This is not to say that there was not always a link between drugs, terrorism and political insurgency, merely it is the sharpening and increased reliance of such groups on illicit markets that has entrenched this nexus (Martin 2015).

Indeed all the major zones which have been associated with the production of illicit substances such as the Golden Crescent in Central Asia, the Golden Triangle in South East Asia plus the Beka Valley in the Lebanon not to mention the Bolivian, Peruvian and Colombian coca producing regions are all conspicuous by their lack of central governmental control and by a symbiotic coexistence between drugs and terrorism.

Additionally, it is worth noting how the above organizations have begun to cooperate with transnational organized crime groups in order to maximize their mutual objectives. FARC has been especially prolific in establishing such ties with both the Russian Mafia as well as with coca growers in Bolivia, Peru and with "Narcotraficantes" in Mexico, allowing them to tap into new international markets by exploiting the communicative and logistical pathways provided for by global interconnectedness (Naim 2005). The implications for security that these business channels and collaborations can pose are evident, when considering that 22%-60% of Afghanistan's GDP is based on the trade of heroin alone (UNODC 2003). The ramifications of drug money being so fundamental to a nation's economy, means that their governments actions are restricted by the damage they must afflict on themselves in order to reduce drug related criminal activity. Subsequently most policies aimed at curbing the drug supply are seldom going to be welcomed by the population at hand, more so by a population deprived of viable alternatives. These trends naturally provoke greater political turmoil, as weak governments attempt to implement unpopular and economically damaging legislation, which have little support amongst the public and therefore are generally unenforceable. Politicians as a rule wish to remain in power and as such are beholden to their electorate. It remains the perennial conflict of interests. It is therefore no surprise that terrorists and criminal gangs seek countries bereft of strong central government control, where corruption is rife due to poverty and social anomie, (Kleiman et al 2011). The good news is that so far drug production has remained isolated to specific regions, (Even in Afghanistan only 3% of arable land is used for the production of poppies (Paoli et al 2009) the bad news is, that given the robust nature of the plants from whence we derive illicit substances, their potential to be grown almost anywhere is great and presents a real threat (Stares 1996). The unexpected entrance of Columbia in the 1980s into the Heroin market as both a producer and exporter is a vexatious reminder thereof as too is the sudden development of a multifaceted illicit drug industry in Mexico. (Guardian 2015)

The forecast given persistent strains related to globalization are not favourable. The possibility that states such as North Korea or Iran may suddenly implode, replicating the demise of the USSR in terms of social dysfunction, from which the transnational drug market could offer those with the opportunity, economic respite is a distinct possibility. The authoritive Andrei Lankov professor of history at Koomkin University Seoul sees a collapse of the North Korean state as entirely likely and draws attention to the 300000-400000 elite professional soldiers that are likely to be drawn into organized crime in the chaotic aftermath that is almost certain to ensue should/when the Kim dynasty finally meets its demise (Lankow 2015). That certain entities within North Korea should seek to enter the drugs market is based on precedence. Not only have North Korean diplomats been caught handling illicit substances abroad (Lankow 2015), even domestically Lankow notes the emergence of a burgeoning designer drug scene, the main staple of which is reported to be "ice" or methamphetamine to give its official title. Lankow paints the all too familiar picture in which drug smugglers in the DPKR like their counterparts elsewhere enjoy opulent lifestyles and are confronted by authorities who are not "too eager" to intervene.(Lankow 2015) Of equal importance are the transnational smuggling networks that have unfolded over the last decades particularly into China, that drug runners could easily exploit. The situation in Iran is similarly precarious, with its 936 km long mutual frontier with Afghanistan it has become not only a hub for the trafficking of heroin, but also home to the world's highest user rates. (Iran has a 5% user rate among the population) and that despite intercepting 85 % of global heroin seizures. Iran since the 1950s has had a zero-tolerance approach to narcotics (Christensen 2011). A policy which however has proved ineffectual even costing the lives of 3500 soldiers since 1979 who gave up their lives in Iran's "war on drugs" (Christensen 2011). Iran historically was also one of the world's largest producing nations. In fact, only India was considered to be ahead of Iran in terms of supply for many years (Paoli et al 2009). Political stability in the face of global change must therefore be deemed as essential in staving off new sources. If this remains possible is another question. The link between failed states or" black holes" and drugs is well established (Naim 2005). As Moses surmised "As sovereignty erodes and nations face growing difficulties in controlling their borders, there

is every indication that the geopolitical black holes
that illicit networks have come to inhabit and cultivate
are only going to expand" (Naim 2005).

Chapter 9

ISIS enter the drugs game

The insecurities generated by civil strife as acknowledged in the previous section, have been seized upon by Islamic state as it forced its way into the power vacuums that followed conflicts in Iraq, Libya and Syria. The rise of ISIS and its subsequent foray into the illicit drugs market therefore comes as no surprise and is atypical of Findlay's assertion that global conflicts have now become dominated by crime as warfare (Findlay 2003). Reports of ISIS involvement in drug trafficking gained traction in 2015 when Italian police and border security identified a new trafficking route that saw drugs shipments originating from ISIS controlled territories in Iraq and the Levant entering southern Italy via Libya (Callimachi & Tondo 2016). Libya has long had established trafficking routes which have provided passage for Cocaine from south America to Europe via West Africa, now it seems ISIS too are seeking to transit narcotics sourced from the middle east along the Libya to Europe transit route (Williams 2019).

Libya has become a prime destination on several accounts, one criminal and terrorist gangs are able to exploit the political and legal void that has followed in the aftermath of the war, there is no effective police presence throughout the country, while the desperation of the local population, has enabled or rather forced those in need to cooperate with organization's they would normally avoid, what is more those elements of law enforcement agencies that have managed to survive in certain areas can be bought (Williams 2019). While the chaos caused by the migrant crisis that followed the NATO bombing and overthrow of Gaddafi invariably provides cover for those who wish to transport drugs hidden among the refugees, meaning detection rates are reduced (Obaji 2018). In sum the chaos released by the conflict has allowed not only the free movement of drugs and other contraband, but also provided fertile ground from which gangs and terrorist groups are able to derive significant profit.

These conditions have been replicated not only in Libya, but also in Syria, Iraq, Afghanistan and to a lesser extent Lebanon and Iran. In his report for the Asia Times Omar Al Jaffal refers to the new social realities that have provided a springboard for the production and trafficking of narcotics. His view echoes those we have addressed throughout this book when citing that "the deterioration of social conditions resulting from increasing unemployment and poverty" have had a significant effect on the escalation in Iraq of the drugs business, Al-Jaffal also points to the high levels of state corruption, not to mention the "weakness of the security apparatus and a lack of training for its personnel, and the absence of rehabilitation center's for drug addicts."(Al Jaffal 2019) Where the Libyan and Iraqi state has succumbed to chaos losing their ability to provide state functions and public services or to maintain control over vast swathes of territory , Islamic state by contrast, due to its fluid nature and autonomous units survives precisely there where the state is unable to impose its authority, irrespective of the large territorial loses the so called Caliphate has suffered in the last years. In this regard DAESH is much more than a state, it is an ideology, that much like populists in the West derives profit from the disaffection that inhabits the void. In this sense Islamic state appears to some degree antifragile, that is an entity that can thrive amidst disorder and unpredictability.

Aware of the weaknesses in a host of failed states ISIS and their affiliates have been adept at cultivating transactional relationships with various nefarious actors across the middle east, the Camorra and Ndrangeta in Southern Italy and groups such as FARC and the NLA in South America (Williams 2019). In their online magazine *Rumiyah* ISIS examined how amid the chaos of conflict relationships could be forged with criminal networks in war torn countries such as the Ukraine and Syria. This ability to connect with other subversive groups has enabled ISIS to dominate the Middle Eastern drugs business, hence providing a means of macro financing. In this regard narcotics have become an increasingly important source of cash, since the ability to tax a large population has by and large evaporated with the loss of most of their territory (Clarke 2017)

Alternatively drugs also provide what Magnus Ranstop a Swedish terrorism expert calls microfinancing, here European autonomous units that adhere to the DAESH ideology raise funds from what one can generally call small time drug dealing, such revenues allow terrorists to travel back and fourth to several conflict zones, but also play a fundamental role in small scale terror attacks, where mobile phones, knives and cars can be hired with the funds (Ranstop 2016)

These European subunits therefore provide an opportunity for DAESH to develop and operate an entire trafficking network from start to finish.

So, what does the scale of ISIS trafficking look like. Naturally it's hard to make an assessment, data collected refers only to successful interdictions or seizures. What we know however indicates the group are involved in major trafficking operations. 21 ships which have been captured by European state authorities have been associated with the terrorist organization and carried a combined total of 295 million tons of hashish, for a combined value of approximately 3 billion Euro (Callimachi &Tondo 2016). While 11 million Captigon (Fenethylline hydrochloride an amphetamine stiumlant) pills a drug closely linked to ISIS fighters were seized at the Syrian borders in 2016 this confiscation of drugs has been dwarfed by a massive interception of the drug off the coast of Greece with a combined value of $660 million (Giorgiopoulos 2019). There have also been multiple reports of Western state authorities intercepting shipments of the synthetic opiate Tramadol with Greek border control seizing 26 million tablets in 2016, followed the next year by Italian port authorities who captured 50 million euros worth of the same substance in the southern port of Gioia Tauro, and another shipment in 2017 in Genoa worth 74 million EUR.

In a 2015 conference the head of the Russian anti-drug agency Victor Ivanov stated that just from Afghani heroin alone ISIS was making up to one billion USD a year (RT 2015). The tentacles of ISISs illegal drug networks span considerable distances. There are several key routes they operate. These include the transhipment of Hashish and heroin from Afghanistan, which may travel via Turkey, through the Balkans then into Europe, then there are the two routes from the Middle East to Libya, one branches off to Egypt then back up through the Balkans and into Europe while the second path goes directly from Libya to the south of Italy. Libya provides a third route that brings 40% of South American cocaine to Europe. This route is the notorious "Highway 10" channel that comes into contact with Islamist groups in Nigeria, Niger, Guinea Bissau and Mali among others. The wholesale value of this Cocaine route is estimated to be worth $1.8 billion (FT 2008)

Highway 10

Highway 10 sees a confluence of two different forms of trafficking, then South American cocaine that arrives in Africa is at times carried by those being trafficked or smuggled to Europe. These illicit movements of both humans and goods therefore form part of the same picture, their consequences equate to the weakening of the regional state due to endemic corruption and the simultaneous empowerment of both the terrorist and criminal actors who service human needs and desires for profit. Highway 10 is also where South American terrorist groups such as FARC and the Colombian right wing NLA conduct their business with Islamist groups such as Boko Haram, Al Qaeda and the affiliates of ISIS. One such affiliate is the Islamic State in the Greater Sahara lead by Adnan Abu Walid al-Sahrawi which gained notoriety in 2017, when an ambush in the Nigerien border village of Tongo Tongo killed four US military personal. According to one eyewitness deals are generally struck in Guinea Bissau between the aforementioned Colombian terror organisations and Islamic State. Payment is arranged with 50% up front and 50% on completion of the delivery, Cocaine itself makes up part of the payment, hence ISIS is encouraged to develop its own networks through which it can push the drug, therefore fears abound in some quarters that the entire route from the Atlantic coast into Europe could be seized and incorporated (Perhaps violently) into the ISIS structure . Certainly, the Islamic organisation s operating in the area have the means and the know how to establish such a cross transnational operation (Obaji 2018) (FT 2008).

Given the gravity of the criminal and terror networks that are forming along this route, not to mention their capacity to expand exponentially due to the weakness of regional nation states the security implications generated from the Sahara region are not to be downplayed. It is not by chance after all that these criminal enterprises have sought out the West African and Sahara region through which to funnel their merchandise. To give context to the problem, a seizure of 600 kg of cocaine found in the back of a car in Guinea-Bissau equated to 10% of the states GDP. When the stakes are so high, where money is in short supply and when corruption is so endemic, there is little moral safeguards to withstand any temptation. It comes as no surprise to learn that international drug traffickers as a consequence have been able to rely upon significant sectors within the country's security apparatus to help facilitate their business (FT 2008).When the police, border security and military have been paid off its clear the war on drugs in the area has been lost. This leaves us in a wholly unfavourable situation. Then even when being able to register successes such as routing out a corrupt police force, we must recognise that a drug cartel will simply move further up the coast. A solution would appear to be handing the job of drug enforcement to foreign forces, it's an idea Matthew Green put forward in his report for the financial times in which he remarked, the international community "mustered large UN peacekeeping forces to restabilise Sierra Leone and Liberia after wars funded by diamonds". This represents a template to follow with regards to the narco business and a recognition that illicit drugs money has a compounding effect in as much as it drives further illicit trade in all manner of sectors, that in turn contributes to a further weakening of the state (FT 2008).

There are nonetheless complications in the deployment of foreign troops, then affiliations of Islamic state will use it to feed into their quasi fascist portrayal of foreigners as infidels or as occupiers. The local elites too may feel uncomfortable about the presence of an international force in their "backyard" one that may not necessarily concur with their interests.

In Libya the situation is more drastic still, any functioning of the state has been reduced to the bare minimum, with those state actors that have a modicum of control complicit in illicit trade. How therefore is it possible to rebuild the states institutions so vital to development when the very chaos that reigns offers powerful criminal and terrorist groups an incentive to maintain disorder? The sum of this analysis has led Matthew Williams to conclude that understanding Libya's descent into criminality, and how transnational criminal organisations feast on the country is to understand the major threat transnational organised crime presents to the world, economically, politically socially and environmentally. It is a threat which we must understand and challenge" (Williams 2019). Here it is important that Western policy makers, especially European policy makers take heed of the approaching risks. It's vital to acknowledge that the kinetics of globalisation signify that the problems in the Sahara or Sahel are not distant, rather interlinked with threats to our own governance. In the worst case scenario the corruption, trade in illicit commodities, drugs and humans will not only weaken distant nations, but there could be a domino effect into the very heart of the West, especially where countries are not able to absorb or integrate successfully the ceaseless streams of desperate migrants in search of a better life.

Chapter 10

Capitalists as drug dealers? The US opioid epidemic in context

Some on the left could argue that the act of selling drugs is the ultimate form of rentier capitalism, then it produces little of social value, in fact the act of drug dealing is equitable with selling harm for the sole purpose of individual profit. Naturally this is a somewhat reductionist, perhaps extreme view to take, however, the act of pushing drugs on the street level is all about the individuals directly involved. The seller, who seeks enrichment and the individual user who seeks personal gratification. In this chapter we present this over simplistic anti-capitalist rhetoric not as a rigid analytical tool, but rather as a means to question the origins of the US opioid epidemic. In this section we address the old Marxist adage that capitalism itself is the harbinger of crime. Contrary to Marx, who posited that the increasing wealth inequalities forced the immiseration of the working class and then resulted in the poor committing crime (Siegel 2006), we open this chapter by asking whether the structural design of neoliberalism, created an environment conducive for major capitalist corporation's to maximise their revenues through illicit means, in other words the social superstructure failed to check and balance capital.

Certainly, todays capitalist societies are not entirely free of state interventions, interventions which aim to redress aspects of societal inequalities. So, it was in 2016 when President Obama called on Congress to release $1.1 billion in order to tackle the opioid epidemic that had been sweeping across the United States for the past decade. The act congress came to pass would be known as the "21st Century Cures Act and consisted of both primary and secondary prevention measures to combat a crisis which Obama surmised as "A disease that touches too many of our communities-big and small, urban and rural- and devastates families, all while straining the capacity of law enforcement and the health care system" (Sarpatwari et al 2017). Nonetheless it is apparent that the devastating opioid catastrophe appears to have been driven overwhelmingly by faults in the structural design of current market ideology, irrespective of the counter measures introduced by the state. The primordial capitalist tenants that have contributed to the North American drug crisis include above all an increased emphasis on profit and shareholder value. In order to quantify this social catastrophe a quick look at the statistics unveils the full extent of the horror. It is estimated that more than 500,000 Americans have succumbed to overdoses during this epidemic. (Humprheys 2018). In fact, more US citizens have died due to overdoses between 2006 and 2016 then died during World War I and

World War II combined. Worryingly this death rate is tainted yet further by the realisation that of the 2.5 million opioid addicts abusing drugs on a daily basis, many more will perish as a result of their drug consumption. (Humphreys et al 2018) At the times the daily death rate averages 120. (RT 2013)

Incredibly a lot of the blame for this US public health crisis has been laid at the feet of multinational pharmaceutical companies. Indeed, the illicit narcotics market in the States has seen a symbiotic relationship between pharmaceutical opioids such as Hydrocodone, Oxycodone, Codeine, Tremadol and Heroin being formed. It's a scenario in which both Purdue Pharma and Johnson and Johnsons among others have been forced to make compensation settlements that reach into hundreds of millions. Mike Hunter the attorney General at the centre of the Oklahoma Vs Johnson & Johnson case, accused the multinational of playing a significant role in "the worst man made health crisis in the history of the country and the state" indicating that the large number of US addicts was not the mere result of iatrogenic s but the result of pushing drugs to those who did not require them (Guardian 2019) Hunter went on to describe how it was "greed" that drove the Pharmaceuticals agenda.

Concurring with Hunters conclusions another lawyer for the state of Oklahoma stated that Johnson and Johnson, "created a need so they could sell to the need" He accused the company of making false claims that its opioid s were safe and effective for long term treatment of chronic pain despite a lack of clinical studies, he added that "It is a man made crisis. The evidence will show this is a drug company made crisis,"

From the court judgement we may conclude_that a pharmaceutical conglomerate has effectively been deemed to be pushing drugs out of self-interest to amass as much profit as possible and to increase its shareholder value to the detriment of its customers. In this chapter we will look at what factors enabled these large conglomerates to get away with such an anti-social sales strategy, how the regulatory frameworks and their oversight failed US citizens. We will examine how the criminal justice system was rendered toothless in the face of these gargantuan capitalist entities. Of interest are also the initial fines that were handed out to the pharmaceuticals, fines that stood in stark contrast to the profits accumulated and as such provided no deterrence to companies deploying aggressive and often illegal sales techniques, in fact the fines appear as nothing more than a state added tax, as if the state itself merely sought to profit from a continuation of this immoral trade, that no criminal charges were pursued against these giant conglomerates only deepens the suspicions. (Sarpatwari, A et al).

As stated above two key elements are apparent, that point to the structural design of our neoliberal economy from which a pure profit orientated culture among the drug manufacturers may have evolved, namely shareholder value and deregulation. These elements are closely identified with the neoliberal accumulation regime that took root in the 1980s. It was a time when the post war social contract, often associated with Keynes was ripped up and greater importance was given to profit. As one of the leading and authoritative neoliberals Milton Friedman encapsulated "the social responsibility of business is to increase profits". Profit maximisation would invariably be linked to what became known as a process of financialization, which drove far greater levels of investment and in turn drove many western states towards a more service orientated economy and away from production. Why this is significant in the case of both Perdue Pharma and Johnson and Johnson is evident by their focus on profit above all else. Grace Blakely in her book Stolen aptly clarifies the dynamics involved, "because neoclassical economic theory assumes that equity markets are efficient, it also assumes that current stock prices are an accurate reflection of the long-term profitability of a company. Investors will base their investment decisions on the amount of profit they expect the enterprise to make in the future, and how much of that profit they expect the firm to distribute to shareholders. The argument for shareholder value therefore proceeded from business' sole aim to maximise profits, this could be done by simply boosting the current share price as the best way to maximise profits". With profit at the centre of Hayekian ideology it becomes clear how deregulation too, would prove necessary to ensure corporations could act freely to aggrandise their revenues.

At this juncture we will delve more into the corporate modus operandi and review the circumstances which they ruthlessly took advantage of (Blakeley 2019).

The changing view of pain

Starting from the mid-1980s US researchers started placing a greater emphasis on pain management. This shift can be traced back to Marilee Donovan et al who discovered that 45% of patients in a surgical unit reported suffering from excruciating pain. Naturally we would all wish to alleviate such suffering and having caught public attention her work encouraged further study. Another pivotal study into pain was the 1990s research paper by Von Korff et al entitled "Graded Chronic pain Status: An Epidemiologic Evaluation". This study appeared to confirm Donovans work, concurring that many patients were suffering from pain unnecessarily, furthermore this pain provoked secondary complications that impaired on an individual's quality of life. As Von Korff concluded "eight percent of adult enrolees in a large health maintenance organization suffered from severe and persistent pain, which "was strongly associated with . . . frequent use of ambulatory health care, unfavorable self-appraisal of health status, and psychological impairment."(Sarpatwari, A et al) Melzack contributed to these initial assessments arguing in his paper "The Tragedy of Needless Pain" not only that thousands of people were stricken by pain , but that when patients take morphine to address physical pain they seldom succumb to addiction, withal he argued that addiction for terminally ill cancer patients was irrelevant. With hindsight Melzack's position set a dangerous precedent (Case & Deaton 2020), then as a result of these findings increased weight was given to pain eradication, which ended with big pharma expediently distributing incredibly powerful and addictive opioids as the solution. A clear linear course may be charted by which this outcome came into being. An influential speech given in 1996 by James Campbell president of the American Pain Society declared pain the "fifth vital sign". The importance of Campbells speech is apparent when one considers its impact on US healthcare, then almost immediately after his prelection the joint commission on accreditation of healthcare organisations developed a set of guidelines for "pain management standards that hospitals and outpatient centres would have to meet for certification"

The culminate effect on healthcare professionals to recognize pain as the fifth vital sign not to mention the new guidelines upon which certification and a right to practice now relied, exerted immense pressure on practitioners to prescribe these legal opiates. Those who did not adhere to the protocols suddenly risked criminal sanction as The Federation of American Medical Boards suggested to US state medical societies that failure to treat pain should be considered an abuse made punishable along the lines of "battery". Simultaneously the Board placated doctors' concerns by assuring them that to administer large doses of opioid's to patients was acceptable (Sarpatwari, A et al).

Given that pain is subjective, doctors in real terms were denied any objective barometer by which to measure either a patient's suffering or their specific needs. Doctors would offer a patient a numeric scale of one to ten and then were practically forced to respond affirmatively to what was in affect a self-assessment. With the threat of sanction and the removal of accreditation should a patient's pain needs not be met, doctors were virtually given little choice but to prescribe highly addictive pain relief. Additionally, the private nature of US healthcare providers means that Doctors were often forced to consider business interests or market dynamics when prescribing, as negative patient feedback could negatively impact their practices As Myles Gart affirmed in his piece for Medical Economics: "Pain is not the Fifth Vital Sign", "physician's in many specialties' have explained that they feel pressure to over prescribe opioids, and do so to attain higher patient-satisfaction scores for themselves and their hospitals." (Gart 2017)

While much is left to be desired by such practice on an ethical level, it's clear that medics are facing a varied set of pressures that practically constrain their choice in real terms. The aforementioned represents not only a concise conflict of interest but also provides substantial evidence as to how economic and market dynamics presided over ethics. A logical outcome resulting from converging factors. On one hand we have reward in the form of financial gain, that can be obtained by simply prescribing, on the other we find the threat of punishment both on a personal and a financial level and finally we see that Doctors were pressured from above to adapt to the guidelines presented by the various associated boards. Choice was clearly restricted as the eradication of pain suddenly became the be all and end all of a practitioner's job, while the risks of the opioid's were correspondingly downplayed (Gart 2017). The drug manufacturers acting in self-interest moved to safeguard the new pro-narcotic stance pouring millions into PR. Perdue Pharma had a head start in terms of marketing strategies, having developed these in the early 60s when running a campaign that promoted the use of Valium (Diazepam). It was a campaign which led to high rates of addiction to the tranquilliser in the United States. Then as today Perdue downplayed the harmful side-effects or the true addictive nature of their drugs. They funded an organization called "Partners against Pain" and created promotional videos such as "I got my life back" in which patients treated with the Perdue branded opioid Oxycontin praised it as a new miracle drug. In another excerpt the chronic pain expert Dr Alan Spanos claimed that the risks of addiction to Oxycontin were much less than 1%. Refuting as Alison Holmes of Dartmouth-Hitchcock medical center describes as thousands of years of evidence to the contrary. A decisive aspect of the pharma industries strategy was to bring so called "Key opinion leaders" on board, these "KOLs" would be highly accredited and respected experts in the field who's endorsements other MD's would not question. One such figure a Dr Jick wrote a one paragraph story entitled "Addiction rate in patients treated with narcotics" the paragraph would become a seminal reference point repeatedly used to whitewash any adverse effects the drugs may trigger. Another influential review by the Boston Collaborative Drug Surveillance team concluded that out of 12,000 patients treated with opioid's only four had succumbed to addiction. Elsewhere suspicions of the habit-forming nature of these drugs were allayed by a new concept in which addicts were described as "pseudo-addicts". These so-called pseudo-addicts were described as looking like addicts in their desperate search for pain relief. With doctors under pressure to meet the pain needs of their patients, these so-called pseudo-addicts were horrifically given enhanced dosages, going from 80 mg to 140mg. At this point it becomes clear the pharmaceutical industry would conceive of any pretense to protect their sacred profits (Wiland & Bale 2018). The new literature on pain relief created advantageous conditions for the drug companies, who now freely targeted medical professionals in order to market their products. Pain management conferences were set up in luxury resorts where doctors would be welcomed with gifts and presented with the latest evidence promoting the beneficial and innocuous use of opioid's as a means by which to ameliorate pain. Beyond the fancy hotels and the gifts used to sway practitioners Perdue pharma as part of their aggressive marketing strategy paid out 40 million

USD in bonuses associated with the sale of OxyContin. Bonuses of $200,000 were given to sales representatives who managed to hit their targets. Giving them potential to earn five times their basic salaries. When such prizes were on offer, one can assume that every trick in the book was used to obtain the "right" result. To give some perspective of the power of the pharmaceutical industry a striking statistic underscores the problems faced by the state, for example in 2013 the marketing expenditure of the ten largest companies on an individual basis was greater than the whole budget of the US Food and Drug administration (Humphrey et al 2018). And when such power creeps into the academic world as seen above, the system morphs into a nefarious conduit promoting self-Interest at the expense of others. As Dr Jason Fung writing for Medium health makes clear "when the evidence base of medicine is bought and paid for, people die. That is how doctors have created this opioid crisis that kills thousands of people. Pharmaceutical companies want to pay off doctors, just as drug lord want to pay off judges and police officers" before sombrely summarising "Unfortunately doctors and universities have been willing participants in this game of killing for profit" (Fung 2018)

Further strategies such as establishing databases in order to identify users for direct and more effective targeting became common place, while on the legal side the companies and specifically Perdue sought to cement their position and more importantly their profits by making use of deregulation and poor oversight. Particularly low patenting standards ensured Perdue was able to maintain market exclusivity for its products. This was achieved by minor tweaking of the active ingredients or by creating slow release forms, that although obvious in the profession sufficed to persuade the relevant legal bodies that Perdue was indeed producing something distinct. The legal bases upon which the Perdue claim rests is the *KSR International Co Versus Teleflex Inc* that although entirely unrelated to the drugs business played a pivotal role in lowering the bar for what could be deemed as obvious and under which conditions a patent may be rejected (Sarpatwari, A et al 2017) .

In their desperate quest for gaining market exclusivity Perdue pharma once more acted to the detriment of their client group. Then the slow release OxyContin which was supposed to last as long as 12 hours in fact wore off several hours prior to the stated time. Leaving those addicted with a void that would need filling. Doctors therefore came under duress to prescribe higher doses that in time too would become ineffective. As a result, those dependent would be forced to seek alternative avenues in order to address their needs (Humphreys et al 2018).

Where patents had expired and where production now became open to competitors Perdue among others managed to bar generic reproduction by using citizens petitions to prevent competition from gaining market access. These petitions focused above all on the claim that the older products no longer met safety requirements. Hence the more established opioid manufacturers were able to maintain their stronghold on the market. (Sarpatwari, A et al)

Tech company helps Pharmaceutical push drugs

On 27th of January 2020 the San Francisco health information company Practice Fusion admitted to soliciting and receiving kickbacks from a major opioid manufacturer, (Perdue pharma) and as a result of a criminal investigation agreed to pay $145 million to resolve the issue, the sum included $26 million expressly for the payment of criminal fines and forfeiture. (Reuters 2020)

The firm was principally considered guilty of running databases which pushed doctors into prescribing opioids. This was deemed to have been done to the mutual benefit of both Practice Fusion and the drug manufacturer who both aspired to create greater demand in order to generate increased profit, as Emma Court reported for Bloomberg "The tool existed thanks to a secret deal. Its maker,a software company called Practice Fusion, was paid by a major opioid manufacturer to design it in an effort to boost prescriptions for addictive pain pills" Again little consideration was given to the target groups wellbeing, as Court goes on to state "even though overdose deaths had almost tripled during the prior 15 years" (Bloomberg 2020)

The Tech firm created patient health records that when accessed by Doctors would suggest pain management for certain client groups, before promoting the prescription of opioid drugs. The database would even create a treatment plan at the click of a button. Given that the system was being used in approximately 30, 000 surgeries across the country and given the opioid crisis in the states it is perhaps little surprising to discover that the system alert went off 230 million times between 2016 and 2019

The corrupt nature of the joint venture over which Practice Fusion presided was derided in court by Assistant Attorney General Ethan Davis "across the country, physicians rely on electronic health records software to provide vital patient data and unbiased medical information during critical encounters with patients.Kickbacks from drug companies to software vendors that are designed to improperly influence the physician-patient relationship are unacceptable. When a software vendor claims to be providing unbiased medical information – especially information relating to the prescription of opioids – we expect honesty and candor to the physicians making treatment decisions based on that information." (DOJ 2020)

While other commentators pointed out the systemic neoliberal structures that inevitably provide fertile ground for such money-orientated practice that at the same time is detrimental to human beings. As a

Dermatologist from Atlanta Jamie Weisman succinctly noted

"It's evil. There's really no other word for it if you want to model electronic health records as a for-profit system and not regulate them as such and force doctors to be on them, it's almost inevitable that they're going to be manipulated." (Bloomberg 2020).

Chapter 11

Big pharma and how the synthetic opioid market increased heroin consumption

With all the evidence we have presented so far, it's clear to see why the number of prescriptions for opioid s had escalated so rapidly from around 76 million in 1991 to 300 million today. Furthermore, the behaviour of all the aforementioned companies helped to cement a symbiotic relationship between the synthetic manufactured opioid s and illegal street heroin. Primarily this resulted as states became aware of the issues pertaining to addiction and driven by a need to act, they simply sought to reduce the number of opioids in their system. Pain management clinics that had thrived due to lax regulation were targeted and as the crackdown in certain states began to reduce supply, addicts were left with nowhere else to turn to but to street dealers. Heroin and the illicitly obtained Fentanyl were the drugs of preference as desperate addicts sought alternatives to satisfy their needs. This swiftly resulted in a surge of drug related overdoses. However, the crackdown was only one aspect that contributed to the dyadic interplay between legal and illegal consumption. Simple economic calculations helped generate what appears to be a Ponzi scheme of drug abuse, that increasingly brought new users into its supply chain, as Humphreys, Caulkins and Felbab-Brown tersely identified in their prominent article for Foreign Affairs which deserves to be quoted at length.

"The liberalization of painkiller prescriptions has fuelled a black market thanks to a straightforward economic calculus. The black market pays about $1 per milligram for oxycodone pills. A typical daily dose for a long-term opioid patient is 100 milligrams, or $36,500 worth of pills a year. Thus, a patient with a $30 copay for a 30-day prescription pays $1 a day for medicines that can then be sold for $100. Those skilled at working the system can obtain prescriptions for hundreds of milligrams a day, either from one doctor or by doctor shopping. Although most patients are not criminals, many criminals pretend to be patients. Furthermore, even otherwise honest people can be tempted into crime when the payoff is that great. Just by lying about a medical condition that doctors cannot verify with any objective test, a patient can obtain prescriptions worth tens of thousands of dollars.
Even for those who truly need the drugs, the black market offers attractive opportunities. A single milligram of pure heroin usually sells for under $1, slightly less than the price that a milligram of oxycodone commands, even though heroin is roughly three times as potent. Selling prescription pills and buying heroin thus lets the user more than triple his or her opioid consumption or, alternatively, keep the

same rate of consumption and buy groceries or pay the rent.
This creates a vicious cycle: addicted people obtain prescriptions, which they sell to others, who become addicted and seek their own prescriptions, which they then sell in turn, addicting still others. This process has driven a boom in demand. Heroin use, which had stayed stable for many years, surged as people who had become addicted to prescription opioids shifted to black market alternatives"
(Humphreys et al 2018)

The above encapsulates the significance weak regulation has had in the US with regards to the drugs crisis. A key part in the problem was played by thousands of so called "Pill mills" which set up shop all across the United States. From these "pill mills" or Pain management clinics rogue doctors were able to prescribe medication for cash with barely any confirmed diagnosis in the patient needed. Of course, the drugs being served out were all synthetic opiates. As the Evidence suggests, millions upon millions of pain pills were flowing through these centres and finding their way onto the black market. Johnson& Johnson not to mention Perdue Pharma have hitherto been embroiled in the opioid scandal, but these dubious vendors were to an even larger degree being supplied by Cardinal Health, McKesson and AmerisourceBergen. And in doing so these drug industry giants completely neglected their duties which under the "Controlled Substance Act" required them to report suspicious orders to the Drug Enforcement Agency (DEA). Suspicious orders are deemed to be those which occur with great frequency or which are seen as unusually large. An example of this is one notorious pharmacy in Kermit West Virginia which ordered nine million Hydrocone pills in two years. That's an incredible amount of opiate based drugs considering the town's population is less than 400. The Kermit case however was a scenario that was unfolding from state to state and provides evidence that the pharmaceuticals were non compliant with regulation. As Joe Rannazzisi the former chief of the DEAs office of diversion poignantly pointed out in a highly proclaimed CBS investigation "this pharmacy just bought 50 times an amount that a normal pharmacy purchases and they are in a town of 5,000 people. You don't know that that's suspicious?" In the interview Rannazzisi is then asked for confirmation of his claim "You know the implication of what you're saying, that these big companies knew that they were pumping drugs into American communities that were killing people?" His reply, "that's not an implication, that's a fact. That's exactly what they did". He then reiterated what many had concluded that these people at the centre of the epidemic were simply "drug dealers in lab coats"

As a consequence, Rannazzisi set his sights on the drug manufacturers, but as his policy started to reap rewards and as big businesses were being fined, the latter joined forces and started to lobby both the higher echelons of the DEA plus congress, placing them under enormous pressure. The legislature the DEA was seeking to enforce was portrayed as "vague" and no longer fit for court. As another witness former DEA attorney Jonathan Novak has testified. A spanner was suddenly thrown in the works and the DEA diversion unit no longer functioned as an investigative body. This in-cohesiveness was further exacerbated when as many as forty-six lawyers working in the DEAs investigative office were hired away by the drug manufacturers. With their expertise these lawyers were able to aid the opioid produces by highlighting the weaknesses in DEA regulations.

But not satisfied with undermining the drug agency, the pharmaceuticals lobbied congress to implement legislature which would "destroy" the DEAs enforcement capabilities. (CBS 2018)

The act that would serve their needs was signed into power by president Obama on April the 19th 2016. It was known as the Ensuring Patient Access and Effective Drug Enforcement Act (Also known as the Marino Act). This statute was the culmination of several years hard graft by cooperate lawyers on behalf of the pharmaceuticals. The period of lobbying to congress cost the industry $106 million and the bill was passed in its third reading.

As the eponymous name clarifies, the principal argument upon which the legislation is based brings us back to the 80s argument which sought to facilitate access to pain relief. Subsequently the DEA would no longer be able to freeze what it considered "suspicious" deliveries of narcotics. This is defined in section two of the act.

"Current law allows the DEA to immediately suspend a registration to prevent imminent danger to the public health and safety. This bill defines "imminent danger to the public health and safety" to mean an immediate threat of death, serious bodily harm, or abuse of a controlled substance due to a registrant's failure to maintain effective controls against diversion.

The bill revises and expands the required elements of an order to show cause issued by the DEA before it denies, revokes, or suspends a registration for a Controlled Substances Act violation. An order to show cause must specifically state the legal basis for the action and notify the registrant of the opportunity to submit a corrective action plan."

While in section 3 further constraints appear thus.

(Sec. 3) The Food and Drug Administration, the Substance Abuse and Mental Health Services Administration, the Agency for Research and Quality, and the Centers for Disease Control and Prevention, in coordination with the DEA, must report to Congress on:

- *obstacles to legitimate patient access to controlled substances;*
- *diversion of controlled substances;*
(congress.gov 2016)

One of the more incredulous aspects of the law, is that it was penned by a former DEA lawyer named Lindon Barber, who together with Rannazzisi had once issued stark warnings to several drug manufacturers and distributors, and who had requested the latter put a halt to their suspicious large shipments to treatment centres. However, within a month of leaving the DEA he started to represent clients who were in litigation with the agency. (Washington Post 2016)

He became a legal champion for the drugs industry,which insisted that the new law would not prevent the DEA from doing their job. Indeed, certain sectors of the industry went on the offensive, for instance the Healthcare Distribution Management Association, which proved influential in helping secure the new legislations claimed that the DEA had been misusing its authority and was targeting drug distributors which made only minor errors in their audits. It is a claim vehemently denied by Rannazzisi, who insists that the DEAs focus was only ever on those who were caught "sending millions of drugs down the street" (Guardian 2016).

Irrespective of the arguments levelled from one side against another, it seems more than logical that any act that inhibits the DEA from freezing deliveries, which seeks to complicate the procedures by which the Drug agency can impede suspicious deliveries or which gives a lengthy right of appeal to the pharmaceuticals during which the delivery of drugs cannot be frozen, will limit efficient anti-narcotics enforcement .

These cogent sentiments were echoed in a report for the Marquette Law Review by the DEA Administrative Law Judge John J Mulrooney who sought to clarify the detrimental consequences the Marino Act would inevitably carry. The most poignant expressions of this impact can be found between pages 5-9 as seen on the following page (Mulrooney 2015).

Co-sponsors of the EPAEDEA promoted the CAP provisions as "provid[ing] the DEA with the clarity to collaborate with the very people responsible for ensuring that [controlled substances] get to the patients who need them without hurting and harming th[e] distribution chain and while clamping down on diversions and abuse."[16] It was touted as "a mechanism for companies[17] who inadvertently violate the Controlled Substances Act . . . to remediate the violation before their registration is suspended and the supply of drugs to patients is interrupted."[18] It was explained that the EPAEDEA would "encourage greater self-reporting of violations," while helping to "ensure that supply chains remain intact for legitimate uses such as the alleviation of pain and illness."[19] One co-sponsor described the CAP as "a mechanism for companies that violate the Controlled Substances Act to correct their practices" before their registration is suspended or revoked, noting that "[e]ven inadvertent violations may lead to suspension or revocation, disrupting the supply chain for the company's prescription drugs[, which] in turn can cause hardship for patients who rely on the company's drugs for treatment and cure."[20] In sum, the CAP was touted primarily as a method to ensure that patients continue to retain access (hence the "ensuring patient access" feature of the bill's cumbersome title) to controlled substances in the event of "inadvertent violations"[21] of the Controlled Substances Act by "companies"[22] in the distribution supply chain.[23]

The stated justification for the CAP is significantly undermined, however, by an absence of evidence in the Congressional Record or elsewhere to support the position that pending administrative proceedings in any way limit even a single patient's access to medication, the purported reason the bill was introduced in the first place.[24] By the terms of the statute, the CAP provisions do not apply to the Administrator's determination regarding an immediate suspension pending resolution,[25] and in every other adjudication, registrants retain their authority to conduct regulated activities until the Agency issues its final order.[26] Stated differently, if a registrant or applicant is served with an OSC but believes that it has made sufficient improvements to its operating procedures to ensure that the transgressions charged do not re-occur (or if it believes that the transgressions charged did not actually occur), it has—and had before the EPAEDEA—the right to request an administrative hearing and present evidence on its own behalf before any sanction can be imposed upon it.[27] Registrants and applicants have always been afforded the opportunity to present evidence of any corrective actions they have taken to ensure that the charged conduct does not continue, including plans to avoid future

Please turn over leaf

transgressions, and the Agency has always considered such evidence in making its final determination on whether to preclude or curtail the applicant or registrant's regulated activities.[28] Similarly, the parties have always been able to discuss the merits of the case amongst themselves, either before a request for a hearing is made or during the pendency of the administrative proceedings, and if an applicant or registrant offers a proposed plan of corrective action and the Agency (through counsel representing it in the administrative proceeding) determines that it is no longer prudent to continue administrative proceedings, then the Agency (the party which initiated proceedings in the first place) is free to seek termination of the case, which the DEA Administrative Law Judge (ALJ) will grant. Inasmuch as DEA administrative proceedings are remedial[29] and non-punitive in nature,[30] a written proposal to correct alleged deficiencies should, of course, merit special consideration by the Agency in its evaluation of the prudence and expense of continuing to seek preclusion or curtailment of regulated activity, but there was no apparent reason for the EPAEDEA to direct that such a proposal be considered and ruled upon in isolation, outside of an ongoing administrative proceeding. If, in the Agency's view, a proposed plan of action merits discontinuation or deferral of proceedings, it is (and has always been) free to seek termination of administrative proceedings at any time, or it can decide by final order that no sanction is appropriate based on all of the facts, including any remedial actions taken and plans put in place. Thus, the EPAEDEA's CAP provisions present as a solution to a problem that did not (and does not) seem to exist.

Furthermore, the CAP provisions create no incentive (and potentially create a disincentive) for regulated companies or individuals to "self-report[] . . . violations,"[31] to correct wrongdoing before an OSC is filed, or even to follow or continue following whatever plan is deemed sufficient to discontinue or defer proceedings once the proceedings are discontinued or deferred. Instead, the EPAEDEA is akin to a state legislature mandating that law enforcement authorities allow shoplifting suspects caught in the act to outline how they intend to replace purloined items on store shelves; allow intoxicated drivers to pull to the side of the road and park their previously swerving vehicles; or perhaps allow bank robbers to round up and return ink-stained money and agree not to rob any more banks—all before any of those wrongdoers actually admit fault and without any consequence that might deter such behavior in the future. Such mandates sound absurd because they would be absurd. The ability to submit a written plan for improvement may provide incentive for registrants to step up their compliance once charges are filed—or at least, outline a plan and promise to do so—but before that time, they can act freely knowing that they can always come up with a convincing plan to fix their problems later and avoid sanction.[32] And, even in cases where the Agency does elect to discontinue proceedings based on a CAP, the statutory mechanism designed by Congress in the EPAEDEA provides no guarantee that the promises made in the CAP will be fulfilled, or for how long.[33] Assurances by the CAP filers are not required, and the EPAEDEA provides no consequences to unfulfilled CAP representations—even in cases where those representations result in the discontinuation of proceedings.[34] The only thing assured by the Agency's discontinuance of proceedings through the acceptance of a CAP is that administrative proceedings will be discontinued.[35] The benefits for industry are plain, but for the public, the benefits are not as clear.

The position endorsed by Mulrooney and Rannazzisi is one which was shared by over 2000 cities and towns which sought to hold big pharmaceutical companies accountable for the opioid epidemic that has hit their residents hard. The plaintiffs pursued their case in a Cleveland federal court under the Racketeer Influenced and Corrupt Organizations act (RICO). The RICO act here is significant then it seems to suggest that an active conspiracy was implemented by the pharmaceuticals to restrain the activities of the DEA. As one of the lawyers representing the plaintiffs argued:the "Defendants carried out their strategy to weaken the DEAs enforcement capabilities in part through the Marino Bill (that is the :Ensuring Patient Access and Effective Drug Enforcement Act) while a further e-mail written in 2007 by Anita Ducca a senior director for regulatory affairs of the Healthcare Distribution Management Association (HDMA) is used as further evidence of a plot. Ducca wrote:

"Given the intensity and impact of the Drug Enforcement Administrations recent actions, and the concerns expressed by the HDMAs executive committee last week, HDMA recommends developing a comprehensive DEA strategy"

Before setting out how she intended to contact "appropriate decision makers" at the DEA and those working for federal agencies which could be supportive of the industry. Once more at the Cleveland trial a familiar name cropped up, that is Perdue Pharma. According to a Washington Post report Perdues then compliance director Crowley wrote to a senior vice president at Cardinal saying that the pharmaceuticals have to "support itself and each other" and that they must "protect itself from overzealous regulators" (Washington Post 2019)

One must conclude that the evidence represented a genuine conspiracy was being orchestrated among the industries top brass. And on the 20th October the pharmaceuticals at the heart of the trial conceded defeat, agreeing to an out of court settlement hours before proceedings were due to begin. The settlement however means the defendants have officially made no admission of wrongdoing and that any evidence associated with the trial will not be aired (AP 2019).

To give this case study a visual context we can look at two graphs produced by the DEA which appeared in the Washington post that may help the reader digest the impact of the EPAEDEA which the drugs industry so desperately sought to pass through congress.

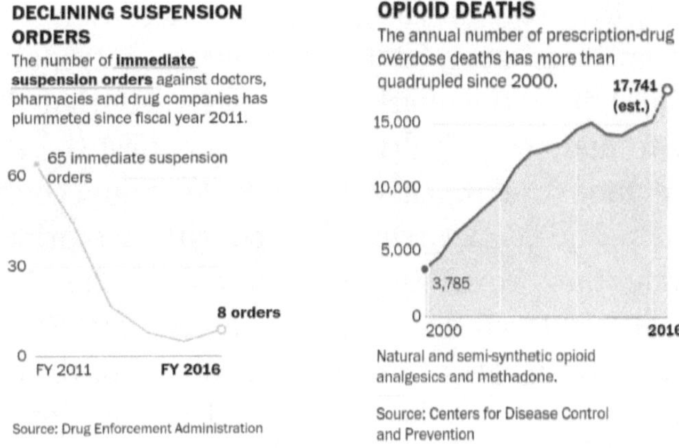

It's clear from the graphs above that the Opioid deaths on the right increased significantly as the DEAs suspension orders declined. The court cases offer the families a sense of justice and yet despite the large settlements paid out by the pharmaceuticals many are still not convinced that the tide has been fully turned against the drug industry. In 2019 a new opioid under the brand name Desuvia was approved by the FSA, leading to disquiet and disagreement between members of various bodies. The drug also known as Sufentanil is a sublingual opioid analgesic that is reported in some quarters to be ten times more potent than Fentanyl, a drug which is considered up to a thousand times more powerful than Morphine. Its little surprising that the FSA decision to approve such a drug in the midst of an opioid epidemic should cause an uproar. In an article in the Guardian Dr Raeford Brown an anaesthesiologist who has been advising the FDA on drug approvals for more than five years was completely opposed to introducing Sufentanil into the market. He reasoned that "the ability to manage that drug once it gets past the FDA is not demonstrated." there's very little, if any, control over them, no matter what the sponsor says prior to the time they come on the market," The drugs approval is viewed as confirmation that the FDA is placing the interests of the industry ahead of those of the people. That people have started to question the agencies transparency is hardly surprising given revelations that the division responsible for giving opioids the green light receives 75% of its budget from the drugs industry. Not only this but officials taking part in the approval process were according to the guardian "taking part in a "pay to play" scheme in which manufacturers paid to attend meetings to draw up the criteria for approving prescription narcotics." Moreover, Desuvia had been rejected in 2017 on safety grounds. That it was resubmitted once more for consideration in 2018 at precisely that moment when the agencies harshest critic of the drug Dr Brown was away on a conference in San Francisco did little to lift the sense of opaqueness that has shrouded the FDA. Yet Dr Brown was only one of a host of the FDA safety committee who had been excluded from the hearing that finally cleared Desuvia (Guardian 2019). The behaviour of the FDA prompted US senators Markey,

McCaskill, Manchin III and Richard Blumenthal to write to the organisation voicing their concerns.

United States Senate
WASHINGTON, DC 20510

October 31, 2018

The Honorable Scott Gottlieb, M.D.
Commissioner
U.S. Food and Drug Administration
10903 New Hampshire Avenue
Silver Spring, MD 20993

Dear Commissioner Gottlieb,

We write to express concern about the application pending before the Food and Drug Administration (FDA) for the approval of Dsuvia, a new formulation of the opioid painkiller sufentanil. In the midst of a national opioid overdose crisis, we are particularly alarmed that, on October 12, 2018, the FDA's Anesthetic and Analgesic Drug Product Advisory Committee (AADPAC) proceeded to convene and vote in favor of approving the application — in the absence of the Committee's Chair, who had expressed serious concerns about the product and opposed its approval. We are also deeply troubled that the FDA's full Drug Safety and Risk Management Advisory Committee (DSaRM) was not involved in the approval process. We urge you to deny the application for approval of Dsuvia unless and until you can reconvene both the AADPAC, with its Chair, and the full DSaRM, to ensure more robust and transparent consideration of the safety of what appears to be a very risky opioid product.

Last year, an estimated 29,000 Americans died from an overdose caused by fentanyl or another synthetic opioid, excluding methadone.[1] Although *illicit* fentanyl laced in heroin and other drugs has contributed to this burgeoning number of opioid overdose deaths, the diversion from medically supervised settings of FDA-approved *pharmaceutical* fentanyl and its synthetic analogs such as sufentanil remains a risk that threatens our ability to respond comprehensively to the opioid epidemic.

Sufentanil is 10 times more potent than fentanyl and 1,000 times more powerful than morphine.[2] Dsuvia's formulation — a small, single tablet administered sublingually — allows for rapid absorption into the blood stream.[3] These properties also make the product highly divertible. Sufentanil has been known for decades to be diverted in its current intravenous form, and whether administered intravenously or sublingually, it can deliver a potency that has been known to be lethal in small dosages.[4] Sufentanil and fentanyl are the two most common substances for

[1] Centers for Disease Control and Prevention National Vital Statistics System, https://www.cdc.gov/nchs/nvss/vsrr/drug-overdose-data.htm (last visited Oct. 25, 2018).
[2] Srihari Tella, Statement before the United States Sentencing Commission for a Public Hearing on Fentanyl and Synthetic Cannabinoids (Dec. 5, 2017), https://www.ussc.gov/sites/default/files/pdf/amendment-process/public-hearings-and-meetings/20171205/Tella.pdf.
[3] AcelRx Pharmaceutical Products, Dsuvia (last visited Oct. 25, 2018), http://www.acelrx.com/products/dsuvia.php.
[4] Letter from Dr. Raeford Brown, Professor of Anesthesiology and Pediatrics at the University of Kentucky College of Medicine and Chair of the AADPAC; Dr. Sidney Wolfe, Founder and Senior Advisor for Public Citizen's Health

which anesthesiologists enter addiction treatment.[5] Because intravenous sufentanil diversion already occurs, it would be reasonable to assume that a small, tablet form of this potent painkiller — such as Dsuvia — would be an even more easily diverted pathway for someone seeking to access sufentanil outside its intended use.

This diversion risk was born out in the clinical trials for Dsuvia, where some tablets were "dropped," meaning that they were not successfully administered to the patient.[4] The FDA recognized this potential for diversion when the manufacturer sought approval for Dsuvia in 2017 and required the company to strengthen its efforts to prevent "use-related errors," which include dropped tablets.[6] But experts maintain that the manufacturer's updated diversion mitigation plan is still insufficient.[4]

Beyond the risk of diversion, we are troubled by the FDA's advisory committee process for this product. This puzzling and unacceptable course of events is unfortunately reminiscent of previous FDA processes and practices that contributed to the opioid epidemic. Some of us have written letters to your agency and raised concerns with you personally about the FDA's historical complicity in the nation's opioid crisis. Some of us have also called on the FDA to convene advisory committees for all new opioid drug application approvals, and have specifically urged the agency to consider addiction, abuse, and dependence in determining if an opioid candidate is safe.[7] For that reason, we are particularly alarmed that, in considering the application for Dsuvia, the FDA did not convene the full DSaRM.

DSaRM review of a new drug application is intended to ensure that, during the approval process, the potential risks of the drug are discussed and considered. Convening a joint meeting of the full AADPAC and the DSaRM would have signaled that the FDA was fully exploring the relationship between Dsuvia's risks and benefits. Not empaneling both committees jointly was a missed opportunity to demonstrate that the FDA is committed to fighting the opioid epidemic and that it has learned from past mistakes.

During 2016 and 2017, in all 11 instances where an AADPAC meeting discussed a specific opioid or opioid issues generally, the full DSaRM was invited as a co-committee.[8] This year, it appears that the FDA has changed this process, to the detriment of public health. The FDA appears to have empaneled, or apparently intends to empanel, AADPAC and DSaRM jointly in

---

Research Group; Dr. Meena Aladdin, Health Researcher for Public Citizen's Health Research Group; Dr. Michael Carome, Director for Public Citizen's Health Research Group to Dr. Scott Gottlieb, FDA Commissioner; Dr. Janet Woodcock, Director of the Center for Drug Evaluation and Research (CDER) at the FDA; Dr. Sharon Hertz, CDER (Oct. 18, 2018), https://www.citizen.org/sites/default/files/2451.pdf.

[5] Ethan Bryson, MD, and Jeffrey Silverstein, MD, *Addiction and Substance Abuse in Anesthesiology*, Anesthesiology (Nov. 2008), http://anesthesiology.pubs.asahq.org/article.aspx?articleid=1922230.

[6] Press Release, AcelRx Pharmaceuticals, AcelRx Pharmaceuticals Receives Complete Response Letter from the FDA for DSUVIA™ NDA (Oct. 12, 2017).

[7] Press Release, Senator Edward J. Markey, Senator Markey Announces Hold on FDA Chief Nominee Citing Concerns with Agency's Failures on Opioid Painkiller Approvals (Jan. 25, 2016).

[8] FDA Anesthetic and Analgesic Drug Products Advisory Committee, https://www.fda.gov/AdvisoryCommittees/CommitteesMeetingMaterials/Drugs/AnestheticAndAnalgesicDrugProductsAdvisoryCommittee/default.htm (last visited Oct. 27, 2018).

The Honorable Scott Gottlieb
October 31, 2018
Page 3 of 3

just six of the nine instances where an opioid product or general opioid discussion occurred or may occur in 2018.[8]

Further adding to the infirmity of the FDA's Dsuvia approval process, the AADPAC Chair was absent the day of the committee vote. It hardly inspires confidence in the approval process when a consequential vote shrouded in controversy proceeds without an advisory committee chair or the voices of the full DSaRM, the committee specifically charged with considering safety and risk concerns.

Finally, the historical ineffectiveness of opioid risk evaluation and mitigation strategies (REMS) and the lack of uniform opioid prescriber education — two important issues some of us have previously raised with you and your agency — causes concern. If the FDA approves Dsuvia and it is successfully diverted, unintended users will face grave risks, and it will be extremely challenging to protect them.

Given the tragic arc of the opioid epidemic, it is imperative that the FDA thoroughly and completely vet any new opioids or formulations of existing opioids through a robust, transparent, and fair process. We do not believe the FDA's process for Dsuvia has remotely met this standard. We therefore urge you to deny the application for this product unless and until there is an opportunity for the Chair of the AADPAC and the full DSaRM to fully consider the Dsuvia application before you take any action.

Thank you for your attention to this important public health issue.

Sincerely,

Edward J. Markey
United States Senator

Claire McCaskill
United States Senator

Joe Manchin III
United States Senator

Richard Blumenthal
United States Senator

Senator Joe Manchin of West Virginia a state terribly effected by the opioid crisis made his position clear "this puzzling and unacceptable course of events is unfortunately reminiscent of previous FDA processes and practices that contributed to the opioid epidemic," Manchin went as far as to suggest that the FDA were "complicit" in the drug travesty. On the other hand a spokeswoman for the manufacturer

AcelRX insisted that "we have much stricter audits and monitoring and controls where we will have oversight from our manufacturers, from our distributors, wholesalers, all the way to the medically supervised setting," She also informed those present that AcelRX has a contract with Denver Health, a firm which runs the RADARS system on behalf of the manufacturer to prevent Desuvia being abused, misused or diverted once it leaves the production site.

Given the incredible power of the drug fears nonetheless persist, as Dr Sidney Wolfe a senior advisor for the NGO "Public Citizen's Health Research Group" confirms when commenting that "it is certain that Dsuvia will worsen the opioid epidemic and kill people needlessly," That such little faith is placed in the regulatory bodies is understandable given the failures that have besieged the US for more than a decade (Guardian 2019). As Donald Trump's commission into "Combating Drug Addiction and the Opioid Crisis" concluded the FDA and other federal agencies did little in the way to adequately regulate either the manufacturers, the distributors or the drugs in question. Therefore, doubts abound especially with regards to Desuvia and the claim of FDA "complicity" in the epidemic appears appropriate (Presidents commission 2017)

As part of our research we attempted to test the premise made by AcelRX that the Sufentanil they produce would not find its way onto the street. We so far came across no secondary evidence that explicitly indicated any form of diversion or street abuse of the drug. Nonetheless within minutes of searching online we had come across a website purporting to sell the opioid. An online chemist called "Healthway pharmaceuticals" was even willing to ship the drug to the UK, claiming that customs posed no problem for their discrete service. Brief research of the company however seemed to indicate that the firm was not entirely trustworthy. The site while appearing professional at first glance, seemed amateurish on closer inspection. There was no contact address or telephone number and the domain was constructed through the web developer "My Blog" available on Google play. No listing for certification or licensing is present. Clearly the site is designed to masquerade as a professional chemist, nonetheless from the exchanged conversation it was apparent that this was not the case, furthermore there was no company registration to be found anywhere. We can assume therefore the web page is designed with the aim of taking part in illegal activity. That the page was found immediately at the top of a bing.com web search in which a wish to buy Sufentanil was given, was somewhat surprising. There was no need to search the darknet, consequently we conclude that the IP address is shielded with a virtual private server.

Within seconds we found another web page "Better Life Meds" this site seemed to be run by the same people as Healthway pharmaceuticals. The product pictures and descriptions were the same, in addition the site offered not only medicines, but also blatantly illegal drugs such as Heroin, Cocaine, LSD etc. While the true nature of these sites has not been established there is clear academic research that points to the sale of pharmaceutical drugs on the darknet (UNODC 2019).

So, there are risks Desuvia could go rogue in the US, after all 90% of globally reported diversions have come from the States. Thefts have been common from manufacturing facilities, from hospitals, surgeries and wholesalers while private prescriptions have at times been sold to unauthorised people. International trade routes equally have been prone to theft. The weakness in keeping Sufentnil in a legal and controlled environment is found in the incredible power the drug expels in very small measures. As Brown in an interview with Rolling stone warned "that regardless of its form, the small dosing volume made it easier to divert and abuse". Clearly at times the drug could be diverted. We assume that even the best preventative measures are permeable. This however is not the main point, rather it's a question of whether a large enough quantity of the drug could be diverted to make an impact on the current epidemic. Time will tell, certainly the fears are not completely unjustified (Rolling stone 2018).

Darklabs

While FDA drug approvals and pharmaceutical diversions have played an undisputed role in the US drug catastrophe, worrying evidence is coming to the fore that underground "Darklabs" are bringing increasingly powerful opioids to Western markets.

Two drugs of note Ocfentanil (CAS nr 101343-69-5) developed by Haung in the early 90s and Carfentanil (CAS nr 59708-52-0) developed by Janssen Pharmaceuticals in 1974 have been discovered in the blood streams of the victims of overdoses. Initially their compounds have been hard to identify, as they are not detected by standard toxicology screening based on immunoassays sensitive to identifying heroin and its chemical compounds, but by employing more refined analysis such as high performance liquid chromatography ion trap mass spectrometry with MS capabilities a host of fentanyl analogues have been discovered. By utilizing UHPLC-Ion Trap_MS to post-mortem tissues and fluids the Miami toxicology department ascertained that Carfentanil was a primary cause in the deaths of 134 out of 500 cases (Baumann 2018) (Zibbell et 2020) (Shoff et al 2017). In Europe too more of these Synthetic opioid receptor agonists have been responsible for deaths .While it is now becoming clear that Fentanyl related drugs are increasingly present among overdose victims, there is a fear that toxicology reports to date may have failed to fully comprehend the extent of the damage they have caused. In this regard Carfentanil represents a horrific threat to the wellbeing of drug users, then microscopic quantities of a drug 10,000 times more powerful than Morphine explain why it is not only so fatal but also astonishingly hard to detect (Baumann 2017). It will be interesting to see if drugs like Carfentanil will revolutionise the illicit market, then the small quantities mean traffickers greatly reduce the risk of apprehension by customs and border police. It seems a win-win scenario for organised crime groups. Such a development could indeed already be under way. In November 2017 a drug bust in Canada seized 42 kg of the drug. The largest seizure of an illicit opioid. Reports suggest that darklabs in China and Mexico are guilty of the illegal manufacture of these drugs. Criminals have been particularly adept at finding information on how to concoct these powerful opioids. They do this by collecting data published in both patents and the research work of pharmaceutical companies. These designer drugs then find their way into the US along the traditional heroin routes from the south (Mexico) or from across the Canadian border in the North (Guardian 2017). These drugs often referred to as Novel Synthetic Opioids (NSO) are used as either standalone drugs or sold as heroin adulterants. They may also constitute the active ingredient in soi disant counterfeit pills (Misailidi et al 2017) . A further example of their increased availability in the US market was a 2017 report in which it was claimed that 52% of seizures involving heroin of less than 1gr in weight contained either Fentanyl or Carfentanil. (Zibbell 2020)

As for Ocfentanil the UNODC report of 2017 recorded its presence across the European continent, where it had been sold in Finland, France, Ireland, Luxembourg, Spain, Switzerland and the UK either as heroin or as a product with which to cut heroin with. It is implicated in deaths in several countries. These include Belgium, Switzerland, Ireland, France, the US and Canada (UNODC 2017)

So while we recognise the dangers posed by the overall neoliberal superstructure in the US and the role this afforded the pharmaceuticals to abuse their position, we must recognise that successive clampdowns to ameliorate the US opioid epidemic, are creating a void that criminal gangs are eager to exploit. It could also be possible that we will witness a change in the illicit market as incredibly powerful but yet minuscule opioids reach our streets. There has been some transnational cooperation in addressing these issues with Chinese authorities clamping down on these "darklabs", (Guardian 2017) nonetheless the battle is only just commencing, a couple of sentences in the UNODC world drugs report of 2019 shed light on current trends in "1998-2008 on average 116 kg of pharmaceutical opioids were seized globally. This has risen rapidly with 203 tonnes in 2017 " It's an increase that can only be described as astronomical. (UNODC 2019)

Chapter 12

How Neoliberalism increases push and pull factors in the US illicit drugs market

Throughout this book we have referred to the role neoliberalism has played in relation to both the universal upheavals generated by the processes of globalisation and its subsequent impact on the illicit drugs market. In this chapter we will look deeper into this economic model in the hope of shedding greater light on its significance, of principle interest will be the manner by which the neoliberal order has withered away the social cohesion of the post war Keynesian compact.

In short neoliberalism is generally viewed as an economic model which promotes competition and self-regulating markets. Consumers in this system are endowed with what is a revision of "democratic choice". Democratic choice here reflects the decisions by which we chose to buy or to sell a product, the consumer rewards efficiency and punishes those companies that manufacture substandard produce. The state's role in this model is to uphold the free market and not to interfere with the flow of competition. Regulation should be minimal and constructed to guarantee the system functions without hindrance. According to the work of the English academic David Harvey there are two concepts of neoliberalism, one he defines as a "a model of societal relations in which government regulation and social welfare guarantees are reduced in order to foster market forces driven by private enterprises pursuing profit maximisation" and on the other Harvey posits a system whose primary concern is to restore the power of the economic elites. It does this by establishing an ideological basis that to all intents and purposes justifies this goal (Monbiot 2016). Phrases such as liberty, democracy and the promise of a utilitarian future embodied in the concept of "trickledown economics" are critical in creating legitimation for the systems design, however since the economic crash of 2008 such claims are harder to give credence too, then money poured upwards to save an economic elite from collapse, while harsh austerity programmes were implemented for the citizenry. In other words, exuberant welfare was given from taxpayers money to corporation's, who were to blame for the crisis, at a time when the welfare state as an insurance for the baulk of tax payers was by and large being reduced (Nicol 2010).

For Harvey this apparent injustice is a logical consequence of our current accumulation regime, one in which notions and principals based on liberty and democracy are decimated in order to sustain an elite power. As given in the example above, where money has not so much trickled down in the system but poured upwards as a direct result of state manipulation of the "free market". This realisation can be construed as evidence of class warfare (Nicol 2010), a claim that the US business tycoon and investor Warren Buffet seems to have corroborated with his controversial quote " There's class warfare, all right, but it's my class, the rich class that's making war, and were winning." (Washington Post 2011) From one standpoint Harveys two concepts of neoliberalism are not exclusive, then the primary theory would inevitably result in what appears to be the latter hypothesis, that is the empowerment of an economic elite. No doubt the neoliberal project may have had class conscious warriors, while others seem to have been genuinely committed to its ideological underpinnings. A commitment to the ideological foundations of neoliberalism were evidently on display during the 2008 vote in the US house of representatives in which 113 Republicans voted against the bank bailouts later introduced by Barack Obama. These Republicans can be considered free market principal neoliberals who adhere to the tenant that any interference on behalf of the state to bail out a business was equitable with the corruption of market competition. Put in more concise terms: In a free market, companies should get punished for their mistakes and as such believers of this view are not driven by class war per se (Nicol 2010).

Investigating conspiracy here irrespective of Mr Buffets comments are in this respect somewhat irrelevant and do not belong to the scope of this work. Neither does it need to be established in order to see the impact financialization is having on our societies.

Several commentators on the left provide strong evidence that the free market in essence has never existed and that both the laissez-faire and neoliberal progeny of neoclassical economics have always relied on a strong centralised state as an enforcer of these particular economic orders. In the globalised world the dynamic is slightly different, here the state is a legalised, centralised and localised conduit that enforces the neoliberal ideology that has been disseminated principally via the Western backed institutions of global governance such as the European Union, the IMF and the World Bank, not to mention the WTO (Slobodian 2018). It is among these institutions of unelected technocrats that we find industrial cabals that have been influential in drafting transnational legal frameworks in the interests of transnational corporations, successfully insulating the worldwide operations of capital by placing them beyond the sovereign state and more importantly beyond the intrusion of democracy (Streeck 2017). As a subsequence a radical shift in power from governments to multinational conglomerates became apparent. The asymmetries of power embodied in this ideology of delimited democracy were further skewed by the introduction of central bank independence from government, this meant that politics became quasi beholden by the interests of the bankers and their investors, forcing above all those political parties of the West into the centre ground, giving electorates no real choice and the resultant continuation of the liberal capitalist status quo (Tooze 2020). This power shift is a natural epiphenomena of the processes of globalisation in which states seek to attract business, by a permanent regulatory race to the bottom, a global economy and free capital flows, allow corporation's to engage in "creative treaty shopping" a process by which they actively seek environments most conducive to their interests in profit maximisation and property rights, not to mention their immunisation from democratic egalitarianism. An example of these dynamics is summarised neatly by the *Laffer illusion* where economic growth is claimed to be obtained only by a state which seeks to lower taxes in order to attract more investment and therefore greater taxes (Murphy 2017)(Stiglitz 2016) . Key to securing these benefits for investors and transnational corporations has been the investor state dispute settlement mechanism written into many trade agreements. ISDS is *"a procedural mechanism that allows an investor from one country to bring arbitral proceedings directly against the country in which it has invested. ISDS provisions are contained in many international agreements including free trade agreements, bilateral investments treaties, multilateral investment agreements, national investment laws, and investment contracts"* (Thomas reuters 2020)". Many see these legal proceedings as detrimental to social democratic concepts of society as

Pia Eberhardt of the Corporate Observatory confirms "ISDS works like a global straitjacket that makes it very difficult and expensive for governments to regulate corporations... It is dangerous for democracy."

The ISDS mechanism is considered by it's opponents to favour corporations to such an extent that no longer can governments legislate against them for fear that they could be taken to court and sued for billions of US dollars. Consequentially states no longer feel able to introduce legislature whether to protect their health services or to protect their environment for fear of facing costly litigation. (Ames 2015)

In his book "Why are the Lambs silent" Rainer Mausfeld describes the legal practice of ISDS wherein large corporations have been able to reduce the regulatory framework of the democratic, constitutional state in a hitherto unimaginable way and with often stark consequences for the living conditions of its citizens (Mausfeld 2019). Again the points made here by Mausfeld aptly correspond with the manner by which US pharmaceuticals were not only able to reduce regulations in general with regards to the prescription of opioids and their manufacture, but also with regards to restricting the actions of the DEA, not to mention the ability to influence congress in passing the EPAEDEA all at the expense of US citizens.

So far our rather negative analysis of neoliberalism, however, has only addressed one side of the harm done in the extended American drug crisis. For the harm generated by neoliberalism is not merely a result of the lax regulation and weak enforcement environments that enabled big business to profit from selling habit forming narcotics, but also in the increasing inequalities inherent to the accumulation regime and its associated social issues. Neoliberalism therefore provides both the push and pull factors that make addressing this crisis incredibly difficult. If the post war Kenysian *pax moneta* was grounded in a compromise between capital and labour with the primary aim of balancing both components against one another via the state, in order to promote greater social stability, the neoliberal order by contrast has come to generate ontological insecurity among the population at large. The long-held belief that consumption, higher wages and full employment were essential for the wellbeing of capitalism were suddenly outdated viewpoints. Full employment in the actual sense would be replaced by Friedmans notion of "natural rate of unemployment" in which he envisioned a free-market that delivers a specific unemployment rate associated with price stability and at whatever level that sat, must be considered the true level of full employment. Business now would no longer be constrained by a responsibility to all its stake holders, that is to its workers, to the community, consumers and the state at large. Instead the new doctrine focused merely on a firms shareholders as if their interests were consummate with that of society.

Employment or rather the lack of it, became a tool by which to dominate, as Michal Kalecki has pointed out. For Kalecki the "political aspects" of genuine "full employment" were inimical to capitalism since the threat of the sack was what made capitalism work. capitalism needs a reserve army of desperate workers who will accept low wages (Kalecki 1943).

Under a regime of full employment, the sack would cease to play its role as a disciplinary measure. The social position of the boss would be undermined, and the self-assurance and class-consciousness of the working class would grow. Strike for wage increases and improvements in conditions of work would create political tension. It is true that profits would be higher under a regime of full employment than they are on the average under laissez-faire...but discipline in the factories and price stability are more appreciated than profits by business leaders" (Kalechi 1943).

The zero-hour contract has its roots in precisely this mindset, but the general sense of insecurity goes beyond the immediate workplace. Just as we have seen previously in the case study of Russia, the processes of globalisation with its emphasis on de-industrialisation, mass immigration, labour arbitrage, (the outsourcing of the industrial base to developing countries where cheap labour is exploited for greater profit) and the ensuing societal breakdown have proven extremely damaging to large portions of the US population. In the US these conditions are reproduced not only in the inner cities, but also in the

Appalachian Chain and the once thriving industrial heartlands, which today are referred to as the "Rust Belt", a term which aptly echoes the decay of contemporary America. Here the working class, have had to contend with mass closures of the US industrial base, often transferred to the Far East, while seeing competition in the form of immigration for what work remains. In keeping with the Kalechiean paradigm it is clear to see why US workers went over forty years without a real wage increase (Desilver 2018). As described in earlier chapters the growing inequalities and sense of abandonment and anomie have placed immense strain on both society and the individual, this in turn has helped drive the US drugs epidemic. After all the epidemic has unfolded largely in the areas of the country that have been most vulnerable to the social and economic upheaval. No surprise then that the Centre for Disease and Control Prevention concluded that those on the lowest incomes were at far greater risk of addiction, overdosing or succumbing to HIV. In view of all the information collected so far, we learn that the poor are often prescribed opioids on a higher dosage and for longer periods of time on average than those belonging to higher social classes. (CDC 2012)

Naturally the social experience defines the psychological factors felt on an individual level. In this regard, economists Anne Case and Angus Deaton attributed much of the increased mortality among middle-aged white Americans to direct and indirect health effects of substance use especially among those with less education, who have faced increasing economic challenges and increased psychological stress as a result.

In their book deaths of despair the economists Anne Case and Angus Deaton aptly describe the socio-psychological factors that have beset large portions of the US population and contributed not only to increased rates of alcoholism, drug addiction, but also suicide. The two authors bring light above all to the increasing economic challenges faced by less educated Americans, who have been unable to adjust to the new globalised world or who have been effectively denied any avenues to success by our current economic order (Case & Deaton2020). Again, we see here a strong correlation with the work of Emile Durkheim, who described the phenomenon of anomie in the social turmoil that followed the French revolution. Key in generating "anomie" is a rapid shift in regulatory mechanisms that occur during periods of economic uncertainty, hence the individual is liberated from the individual social restraints that control wants and social desires (Morrison 2001).

Case and Deaton reveal that the USA is an outlier in terms of Middle-aged mortality rates. While the rest of the OECD (Organisation for Economic Cooperation and Development) countries have seen a year on year reduction in death rates between the ages of 40-55 the USA has suddenly seen a sharp upsurge. The opioid epidemic has proven to be a significant factor in this reversal. Our work so far reveals one very distinct paradox, on one hand the US leads the world in the war on drugs, while on the other its commitment to neoliberalism has undermined this very struggle at home, with dire consequences for its domestic population. For Case and Deaton history has shown that drug abuse is related to some form of disruption or disintegration in the users lives. They cite the case of US soldiers who returned from Vietnam as heroin users, but once they return to their old routines and ways of life, the vast majority seem to have kicked their habits easily (Case & Deaton 2020). Social disaffection therefore poses a likely etiology for the drugs epidemic and in contemporary America we see ample evidence to back up this hypothesis. The foundations for this disaffection one can surmise are attributable to unfulfilled social expectations. Again, as our earlier work has shown, particularly in relation to Mertons strain theory, the US has positioned itself as a meritocracy in which all its citizens strive to live the "American dream". The American dream is a promise according to which every citizen irrespective of class or race can attain a prosperous and successful life. It is a condition satisfied not through nepotism or bribery, rather through good honest hard work and sacrifice. It is a dominant cultural myth long associated with America (Investopedia 2020). Indeed the thirty glorious years of economic prosperity that followed WWII suggested this was not myth but reality, however as the Fordist-Kynesian compact faded into the background and was replaced by the current shift in the social-economic contract, the state was no longer able to provide the social mobility to keep the dream alive. Subsequently Merton's notion of strain fills the void between expectation and a lack of opportunity provided by the system. Those who fail to attain success often fall into two categories, those who blame themselves for their own failings and those who believe the system is rigged against them (Case & Deaton 2020). Both paths have dire consequences not only on an individual level, but also in the immediate social vicinity, not to mention for the wellbeing of the state at large.

The principal elements of neoliberalism it seems corrode away at the traditional American way of life. Gone is the prospect of a steady job one could take pride in. Education and health care became increasingly inaccessible. The white working class the central theme in Case and Deatons work now faced stiff competition in cheap labour provided by immigrants or automation. As immigrants flooded into the work force, the unions became increasingly weakened, memberships began to fall. Without the union's workplace benefits dropped away or employers outsourced labour to agency workers therefore saving themselves from having to make benefit or healthcare contributions. Domestic labour suddenly became an expensive option. While in many cases industry just shut up shop and moved overseas altogether, where there was amble supply of a yet cheaper less represented and more vulnerable work force. All these factors have contributed to wage stagnation. Wage stagnation which contrasts sharply with an elite that continues to prosper. For instance, the median wage difference between those without and with a BA degree increased from 40% in 1980 to 80% in 2000 (Case & Deaton 2020). This in an economy that provides little in terms of growth and which therefore applies increasing downwards pressure on the yet more exposed workers. As Case and Deaton illustrate GDP in the post-world war era was 28% higher between 1950 and 1960 per person, by 1970 it was 75% higher than it had been in 1950. While today annual growth is lucky to reach 2% (Case & Deaton 2020).

This reduction in growth has been accompanied by a simultaneous change in the management model. Corporations have ceased to retain staff and invest in innovation, preferring instead to downsize and redistribute from workers to executives and company shareholders. As a result, productivity is impaired and where workplaces are salvaged wages fail to grow.

Additionally, a disconnect has taken place between those at the top of a corporation and those at the bottom. Previously a gifted worker could work his way up to the top. This is no longer possible, indeed with all likelihood the worker at the bottom probably belongs to an agency and thus is not even part of the business. While in the past where opportunity was lacking a worker could move to a different city and start over, the financialization of the global economy and changes in property law have even denied those from struggling communities an opportunity for escape, since the cities have quickly become islands of wealth, far too expensive for many of those who have fallen behind. At every turn the doors are locked for those from the traditional working class (Case & Deaton 2020). For many the great recession of 2008 was a breaking point. Case and Deaton explain that many of the working class considered that all the excuses they had been told to justify the free market and its concept of trickledown economics had been exposed as untruths (Case & Deaton 2020). The elites continued to prosper and at the expense of the rest. The psychological and material wellbeing of the uneducated and working class was sacrificed in order for the rich to gorge on free money. They ascertain that "Large parts of the American economy have been captured to serve the wealthy with the consent and connivance of government. The problem with inequality is that so much of the wealth and income at the top is ill-gotten. Or put another way, the problem is not that we live in an unequal society but that we live in an *unfair* society" (Case & Deaton 2020). Having established the compresence of ontological angst, wage stagnation, lowering living standards plus cognizance of an immoral and unjust economy, it is hardly surprising that many would succumb to anomie. That a society predicated on what by historical standards must be seen as an extreme form of individualism, should be beset by an opioid pandemic cannot be viewed as unsurprising, the traditional institutions that once would have offered people stability such as the church, employment, the unions or the family unit have simply disintegrated. With these support networks gone and a diminished welfare state no longer capable to act as a guarantor of individual security, it becomes natural that alternative coping strategies must be devised. Hence, we must conclude that the opioid misuse that drives the US epidemic is an attempt on the part of many to fill a void left gaping from the socio-economic dissatisfaction of contemporary America. Unfortunately as discussed elsewhere in this work, drug misuse perpetuates further social pathologies, the drug user is held hostage, beholden by what Richard Du Pont calls the "selfish brain" In which the user will neglect not only oneself, and work but his family unit and society at large all in the constant pursuit of securing the consumption of the drug (Du Pont 1997). Such behaviour in a family setting will impinge on any household, leading often to its breakup, which in turn can generate yet more damaged individuals. As witnessed by those who work for social services, drugs tend to lead to an irresponsible lifestyle where dysfunctional childbearing perpetuates further generations of maladjusted individuals with lower resistance to drug use, social norms that would otherwise be embedded in an individual are absent or entirely corrupted. Males as a consequence become less appealing as long term partners, correspondingly they become less marriageable, less employable and therefore more likely to add to collective instability. In a lecture given by the renowned clinical psychologist Jordan Petersen the plight of such men is addressed in detail. For Petersen such men are considered low in the dominance hierarchy, hence are often rejected by females, their status is simply not good enough. The higher a man is in status the more resources are at his disposal. At the bottom of our current social structure anything abnormal is a disaster. People therefore at the bottom hate being at the bottom and as a consequence they die a lot sooner. Relative status is important. Men hate relative poverty and being low in status. Especially where ideas pertaining to meritocracy are engrained in the socio-cultural discourse, here failure is viewed as incompetence. Conversely serotonin levels go up for those of a higher status, insulting them from less negative emotion per unit of uncertainty. They are hence not only happier, but less likely to be afflicted by pain and of course much more able to provide for their families. These men naturally are more attractive to females not only on account of the stability they provide (Petersen 2018). For such Beta males the illicit drug market serves two potential escape routes. One a man may seek to push drugs earning not only financial reward from doing so, but also street credibility and enhanced status, alternatively a male might retreat from society altogether by misusing narcotics. The individual's plight is accentuated by the neoliberal superstructure then it generally deprives low status men any form of institution which can help redress contemporary inequities. As Edin et al noted in their research "work, family, and religion have traditionally played an important role in furnishing working-class Americans with economic resources, moral guidance, and opportunities for civic engagement. Ongoing attachments to work, family, and religion connected working-class men to social bonds and defined identities that kept them in the formal labor market and forestalled health problems. Conversely, precarious attachments to these key social institutions, we argue, may now dilute their power to shepherd and shift men's trajectories and may place them at risk of a host of negative outcomes" They argue that tenuous links to the aforementioned institutions were conducive to "anomie," or "normlessness" a precursor for societal breakdown. While their work focuses predominantly on men in crisis, for women a clear lack of suitable partners may induce low status women to rear children out of wedlock simply to satisfy a cultural vision of womanhood and self-fulfilment. Given the consequent economic hardships associated with such a choice, it is clear that new cycles of despair are likely born concurrently with children born into such realities (Edin et al 2019).

In search of a solution

The work we have covered so far reveals an interesting paradox. On one hand the USA is the driving force in the international war on drugs and on the other they have allowed not only their states but also their citizens to be overrun by powerful opioids. This poses some uncomfortable questions for policy makers as they seek to combat the illicit drugs trade, moreover in terms of the social issues the American case study, as indeed the Russian one, correspond closely with the work of Durkheim who's theory of anomie offers a terse explanation of the disaffection wrought by neoliberal globalization in many contemporary nation states. Key to this disaffection is the intrinsic sense of normlessness the economic model evokes. These components combine to produce both the push and pull factors which provide a fertile breeding ground from where the opioid epidemic sprung. Troubling however is the realization that many strata in US society have been historically prone to these social pathologies and as such have succumbed to waves of addiction. Such waves have included the opioid epidemic that took hold in the South following the defeat in the US civil war , the drug abuse that followed the California gold rush, where the opium dens attracted the many Chinese immigrants who had come to the US in search of work, in the 70s American GIs became hooked on heroin in distant Vietnam before returning home and in the eighties we have seen briefly how the Crack cocaine epidemic surged through several urban Afro-American communities in the 80s. One communality that links these drug epidemics is the massive social transitions which had afflicted the people at the time, equally clear is the manner by which their security and stability had suddenly been completely undermined. During the current epidemic however, there is one marked difference, the epidemic has principally been driven not by an illicit market in the first instance, but by pharmaceutical companies exploiting and bending the legal structures to their advantage.

A pull factor for drug use therefore appears to be rapid transformation and its ensuing disorientation in the day to day lives of our communities. Naturally those communities most vulnerable and least adaptive to social transformation are more at risk of anomie and its manifestations. Of course, change is inevitable, but we can redress the social pathologies by insulating communities from the extremes of financialization and its inherent economic swings. Key in this respect would be to reduce social and economic inequalities and to restructure and entrench once more the social institutions which are vital to societal cohesion. Central to Liberalism is its claim to equal opportunity, since the 80s, most prominently during the financial collapse of 2008 and throughout the coronavirus pandemic this liberal claim has proven an illusion. The re-emergence of a genuine meritocracy could do wonders to reduce communal strain. As Edin et all recognize "society has faced shifts in the relationship of men to work, family, and religion before" (Edin et al 2018) And while there is a yearning for the past among many, it is inconceivable that we may return. To redress the perceived social injustices that bedevil the modern era, to help reorientate the working class and give them a sense of pride or oneness would make society in general more robust. Durkheim as far back as the 19th century substantiated the importance of fairness in the smooth running of the state when proposing "We need to introduce greater justice into their relationships by diminishing those external inequalities that are the source of our ills." Edin et all referring to Durkheim's claim concur "To ease the crisis of working-class men in labor force attachment, ill health, and mortality more than a century later, we may need to do the same (Case & Deaton 2020).

As with every shock the current coronavirus pandemic enables states to restructure their systems. As Milton Friedmann notoriously remarked "only a crisis - actual or perceived - produces real change. When that crisis occurs, the actions that are taken depend on the ideas that are lying around. That, I believe, is our basic function: to develop alternatives to existing policies, to keep them alive and available until the politically impossible becomes the politically inevitable."(Friedmann 2009) and while Friedmann was an erstwhile proponent of the neoliberal cause, the tenant remains a constant when seeking any deep rooted political reorientation. As such we currently find ourselves at the cusp of such an opportunity. The coronavirus has explicitly shown once more that the free market is anything but self-regulating and that it is far from resistant to shocks. As in 2008 the state has had to conduct massive interventions to salvage what could be saved from the pandemic's fallout. The core ideological underpinning of the neoliberal paradigm hence has been proved a fallacy. This realisation enables us to redress increasing inequality by once more installing the state as an arbiter between labour and capital. Especially since governments have practically "nationalized" whole sectors of their respective economies. What is more states might place renewed emphasis on being more self-sufficient, especially as the pandemic during its early stage's in the EU explicitly showed that nations could not always rely on international supply chains or on the help of other countries (Prodi 2020). This would mean peeling back somewhat on the current globalization philosophy. Staples could be nationally produced, while luxury and novelty products and other consumers goods, could continue to rely on global supply chains. This could together with government spending help revive local manufacturing. Additionally, laws could be introduced to ensure that not only shareholders gain from company profits, but the workers too. Linking wage increases to productivity could be perhaps more beneficial to firms as the current practice of rewarding managers with shares in the company, a practice that unifies the interests of the manager with those of the shareholders. (Blakeley 2019)

The reterritorialization of tax along with some capital controls could help prevent wild swings in exchange rates and ensure that governments are no longer pressed into the proverbial "race to the bottom" a scenario in which reduction in tax rates inevitably lead to austerity during periods of crisis. Capital controls would also remove the threat posed by bond vigilantes. These vigilantes would ensure that states adhered to investor friendly polices by threatening capital flight, as a consequence limiting the state's democratic and administrative options. Capital controls backed up by stricter banking regulation would remove the current dilemma. (Blakeley 2019)

Further the senate could place a cap on lobbying, thus preventing certain sectors from dominating the political discourse, hence generating greater balance. In a system where cash plays a significant factor in swaying the political process, it is hard to speak of a true democracy. Redressing the imbalances would go a long way to legitimising the machinations of government. And bring people closer to the centre of power. This could to some degree help people awake from their current stupor (Case & Deaton 2020).

Addressing the more technical aspects of the pharmaceuticals there is need for a new agency such as the UKs NICE to oversee not only regulation, but also the suitability of any drugs that may gain access to the market. The agency would have to be independent and not rely on funds from the industry as it currently does. This is essential then blatant conflicts of interest not to mention the lack of transparency, are clearly detectable among the population at large and as such are corrosive to the concept of a meritocracy. A veneer of respectability demands an end to such corrupt practice (Case & Deaton 2020).

While additional support needs to be provided in order to treat those dependent on drugs. Swiss style safe injecting rooms, with clean syringes and trained medical staff are available not only for a user's physical wellbeing, but where drug users can find and build trustworthy social networks they can rely on.

In Russia we have seen how a religious revival rose amid the transition from communism to capitalism. Perhaps such a transformation could offer US workers a further source of stability. Before working men return to traditional religious institutions, we take the view that employment, wage and policies addressing the increasing inequality currently experienced in the US are put in place. The material needs compliment the spiritual in that it offers greater social coherence from which an individual is freed from satisfying his/her immediate needs for survival. A good general place to start would be a rejection of free-market individualism, with the state making a greater commitment to industrial policy with an emphasis on production, this should be complimented by public investment in infrastructure. Together these elements create a sound base for a working-class revival. The human species is a social being, hence it appears logical that excluding people from the good life will have negative consequences for those banished to the periphery. To reverse this process and generate a more inclusive society with greater opportunity and social mobility can only be beneficial for the overall wellbeing of the national community. And while we address structural issues the United States could implement to reduce push and pull factors that help drive the North American drug experience, we must also consider the legal context of drugs and security in the globalised world. Then while the US epidemic among the OECD nations is an outlier, problems related to narcotics are an issue everywhere in the world. So, this section ends with a caveat then depending on the result we wish to achieve, the above in conjunction with prohibition may not be enough.

Chapter 13

US epidemic to go global?

Throughout this book we have addressed the social issues arising due to globalisation and its accompanying sense of dislocation, furthermore we have examined several factors inherent to our economic model that enabled large drug firms to exploit lax legislation in order to maximise their profits. The court rulings in Oklahoma vs Johnson & Johnson, the various cases brought against Perdue pharma not to mention Vermont vs Practice Fusion. All of the above strongly suggest that on a managerial level conscious decision's were made to push addictive medication irrespective of the consequences for either the social or individual body. Again, shareholder value and market competition all in the name of securing revenue appear to have played the primary motivations. The stance or morality of the pharmaceuticals is equitable with those of the street corner drug pusher. So far we have examined the role pharmaceuticals have played in generating a drugs epidemic in the US context, however in a globalised world, in which neoliberal economics is preeminent and where the same social pathologies are likely to arise, will we have to deal with a universal contagion? It is a theme Humprheys in an article for Foreign

Affairs magazine entitled "Opioids of the Masses: Stopping an American Epidemic From Going Global" addressed (Humprhyes 2018). He came to the disconcerting conclusion that the marketing strategies deployed by the US drug firms within the North American market were now being extended into Europe and Asia. Catalyst for this new orientation is partly driven by a fear among the conglomerates that any tightening of the legal straight jacket in the US will effect profits and of course shareholder value, therefore Humprheys argues the multinationals will seek legal loopholes overseas in nation states unprepared for the challenge, thus provoking what could become a global "public health disaster of historic proportions" (Humphreys 2018).

These fears are not allayed when considering recent research conducted by the 2019 European drug Report. The report notes that since 2009 forty nine new synthetic opioids have entered the continental "street"market as indicated in the graphic below.

(Please see following page)

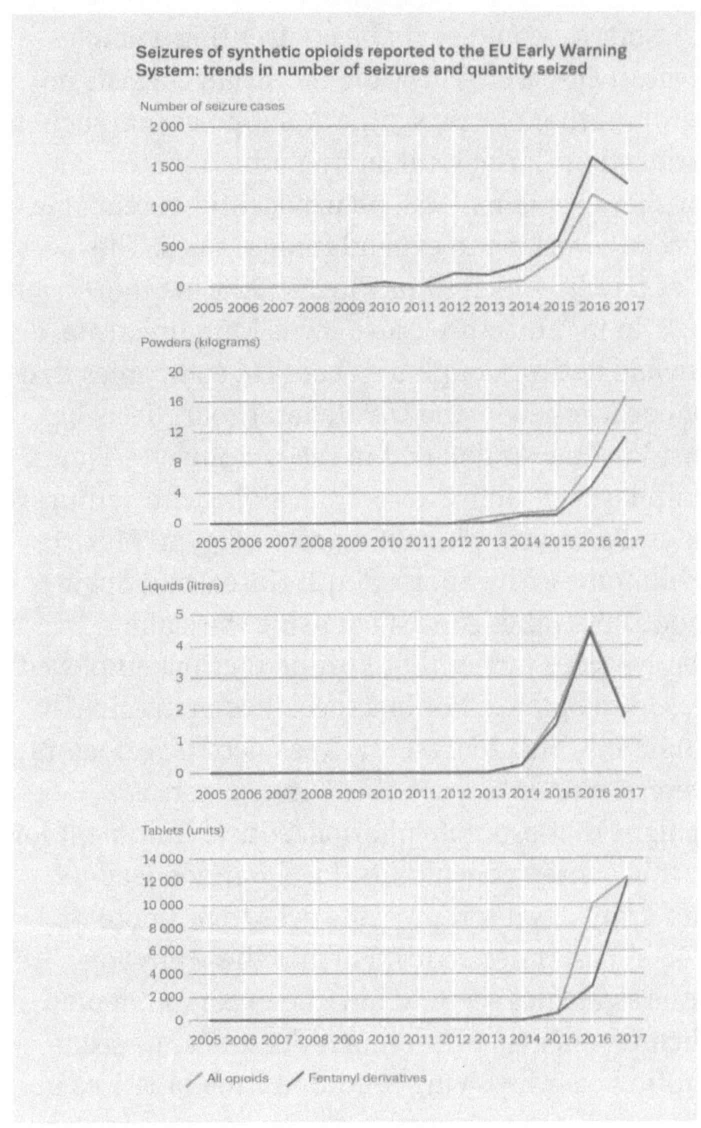

The evidence is clear. Europe today much like in the 1970s when it succumbed to a heroin epidemic that at the time many considered to be a social ill confined to

North America could again be confronting a new "American Disease". This time the strain consists not of Heroin rather of new synthetic suppressants such as Fentanyl or Carfentanil among other opiates. As Humprheys explains "U.S. pharmaceutical companies are already working to expand foreign sales. The Sackler family, which owns Purdue Pharma the Oxycontin manufacturer, also owns Mundipharma, a worldwide network of pharmaceutical companies that is not constrained by the U.S. federal court decision against Purdue. As detailed in the Los Angeles Times, Mundipharma is active across the globe with ventures in Australia, Brazil, China, Colombia, Egypt, Mexico, the Philippines, Singapore, South Korea, and Spain. Its modus operandi consists of using the same aggressive sales tactics that Purdue Pharma employed in the United States. For instance, it runs training seminars in which representatives encourage doctors to overcome their "opiophobia." It sponsors ad campaigns that promote pharmaceutical treatment for pain. It has hired consultants, local opinion leaders, and an army of sales representatives to promote its products" (LA times 2016). Further these already dubious strategies seem to have been complimented by illicit payments to prominent doctors as a recent corruption case involving Mundipharma practices in Italy has indicated. Central to the Italian case is one Dr Fanelli, a consultant in pain management who, it is alleged, has received money from a group commonly referred to as the "Pain-league". In exchange for cash Fanelli effectively championed the pharmaceuticals opioid sales.

Reports claim that as far back as 2009 Dr Fanelli was meeting with representatives of Mundipharma. The year here is of significance, then Dr Fanelli is considered to be the driving force behind a 2010 law which he co-authored, and which allowed for the easier proscribing of opioids. The legal loosening of safeguards against synthetic opioid abuse, however, appears only one of a myriad of strategies deployed by Dr Fanelli, who in addition organised conferences and wrote papers in support of the use of pharmaceutical opioids while downplaying the risk of addiction (Chicago Tribune 2019).

Andrew Kolodny, an executive director of an NGO which advocates for the responsible prescription of opioids, seems to confirm the above mentioned fears when stating that Mundipharma are "using the same play-book that worked in the United States despite knowing it led to a public health catastrophe". Considering the prescription opioid crisis has led to the death of 400,000 users in the States and simultaneously abetted the illicit heroin market, it is vital that governments take heed of the US experience and establish legal measures to protect themselves. The question therefore is: is Europe readying itself for the challenge? (AP, Galofaro 2019)

The indices provided by the graphs above suggest not. Indeed, a report from May of 2019 by the NGO "Corporate Europe Observatory" highlights the undue attention with which the European Commission interacts with the pharmaceutical industry. In fact pharma's main lobbying group EFPIA sits on eight of the commissions advisory boards helping to create an environment conducive to profit maximization, that is to the detriment of health concerns. As the report notes: "EU decision making on public health care and patient rights must be better protected from the influencing attempts by pharmaceutical companies and their lobby groups. Conflicts of interest rules and appropriate "firewalls" which guard against undue influencing of EU policy makers by pharma lobbyists would be important starting points".

The NGO nonetheless is not resigned to defeat, and it places it's hope in the newly adopted Euro parliaments and Commission. If the new Commission, unlike its predecessor, will manage to extrapolate itself from the pharmaceutical industries lobbying groups (who spend somewhere between 40-90 million euro a year targeting the EU) remains to be seen (Corporate Europe Observatory 2019). Certainly, there has been an exponential growth in globally seized pharmaceutical opioids. Between the years 1998-2008 police and border security were on average confiscating 116kg of pharmaceutically produced synthetic opioids, which had been diverted for street use. By 2016 this figure had risen to 205 tonnes an increase of more than 1700% (UNODC 2018).

In Europe reports have steadily been coming through from across the continent that point to this growth. In Sweden it is reported that opioids can be bought from both the conventional and dark web. Nasal spray's containing Acrylfentanyl, plus e-cigarettes or vapes laced with fentanyl have come to the attention of the authorities, while the UNODC worlds drug report of 2017 highlighted the availability of a synthetic opioid 2.5 times stronger than Fentanyl had been identified in Belgium, Finland, France, Ireland, Luxembourg, Spain, Sweden and the UK, with the drug being cited as responsible for drug deaths in Belgium, Switzerland, Ireland, France and further afield in the USA and Canada (UNODC 2017).

With these new threats lingering on the horizon it becomes imperative that governments take heed of the warnings and lessons learned from the US experience.

Chapter 14

State sponsored vigilantes? A Case Study of the Philippine war on drugs

The global war on drugs has at times provoked extreme reactions against certain groups of the world's population, often it is the disadvantaged that have been exposed to any putative measures. In the Philippines this "war" has brought violence and bloodshed to the streets of the country's cities and towns. The nations notorious leader Rodrigo Duerte perhaps more than anyone else personifies the semantics associated with the term "war" in the war on drugs. On his initiative the country has taken a genuinely deadly zero tolerance approach to the nation's drug problem. It has been a strategy that has brought international condemnation of his government.

An important factor in relation to the Philippines battle with drugs is its unique topography. Situated in South-East Asia the Philippines is an archipelagic country consisting of more than 7500 islands. The nation finds itself at a maritime crossroads bounded by the South China sea to the West, the Philippines sea on the East and to the South the Celebes Sea. It has the world's fifth longest coastline; its islands are mountainous and covered with dense tropical rainforests. Economically the nation has taken great leaps forward, by vastly reducing its debt and positioning itself as a creditor nation. The processes of globalisation nonetheless have brought with it the associated social transformations that we have addressed throughout this book, many of the country seek their fortune abroad and as such many family units have been decimated. Urbanisation is increasingly replacing the traditional mechanical agrarianism that dominated the country's economy for most of its history. These developments have contributed to a marked inequality, with tensions arising between the "have's and the have nots". An IMF report of 2006 concluded that 45% of the population are living on less than $2 a day, in congruence with other highly stratified societies, the nation is typically beset by high levels of corruption, marked domestically by what is referred to as the "Padrino system" (Padrino signifies patronage) according to which upward social mobility is based on family affiliations and cronyism rather than merit. The nations porous borders, plus its mountains and jungles added to its societal strains leave the country vulnerable to transnational organised crime. These vulnerabilities were exposed at the beginning of the 1980s as Methamphetamine (Locally know as Shabu) smuggled in from China started hitting the market. In the Philippines distribution of the drug takes place in a less hierarchical and structured manner compared to most other nations, where drugs are often sold by criminal gangs, rather Shabu is distributed along horizontal lines by those occupying menial jobs.

According to local correspondents Coronel, Padilla and Mora working in conjunction with the Stabile Centre for Investigative Journalism " Peddlers here are ordinary men and women for whom selling tiny sachets of meth is more akin to a side business, like hawking cigarettes or newspapers to help pay for food or school fees" (The Atlantic 2019).

According to the UNODC 2012 World Drugs Report, the Philippines had the highest rate of methamphetamine abuse among all the countries in East Asia; The report stated that 2.2% of Filipinos between the ages 16–64 years were methamphetamine users (UNODC 2012)

Corrupt officials and foot soldiers within the Philippine National Police contributed to the problems by seeking to profit from the drugs trade, expediting shipments of narcotics and taking an active role in their sale. Philippine law in conjunction with the patronage system combined in cementing this corruption, by allowing local officials to appoint and dismiss local police commanders according to their whim, allowing profligate city mayors and police to racketeer and enrich themselves. This has lead observers to "compare the PNP to police forces in Al Capone,s Chicago of the 1940,s" (Global Security)

The Philippine drug war began on the 30th of June 2016 the day President Rodrigo Duterte assumed office. Throughout his election campaign, he had promised a harsh crackdown on the drug scene, aligning himself with the South-East Asian country's traditional hostile attitude towards drug addicts. In Gideon Lascos work on drug use in the Philippines this belligerent stance to drug users is charted back to the early 70s when some Filipino bishops referred to addicts as the "worst saboteurs", deeming them "worthy of the highest punishment". Lasco also presents a 1988 Supreme court decision in which one of its decisions expressed that it is "common knowledge that drug addicts become useless if not dangerous members of society and in some instances turn up to be among the living dead" , but perhaps of greater significance are the anti-drug posters and placards that litter the cities and engender hostility towards what has become a dehumanised drug abuser (Lasco 2108). It's a sentiment the president frequently taps into. At a speech in Davao city Duterte told reporters he had been portrayed as "some cousin of Hitler" adding "Hitler massacred three million Jews, now there are three million drug addicts. I'd be happy to slaughter them all" He speaks of drugs as being a scourge on the nation and about wanting to "finish the problem of my country and save the next generation" (BBC 2019). In order to do so he has called on the criminal justice system "to put an end to the drug menace" therefore one of Duterte's first moves was to purge key elements in the security forces, he started by removing police chiefs who were accused of protecting drug dealers. The reshuffle saw a change in 7 out of 12 station commanders. Secondly, he sacked policeman who had allegedly been extorting cash from drug personalities, replacing them with those he felt could be trusted at the forefront of the war on drugs.

The reshuffles brought also increased wages to help fight against bribery (The Atlantic 2019). By August a second wave of dismissals was under way, this time Duterte targeted more than 150 judges, mayors, lawmakers and military personal to the narcotics trade. In a televised address he openly named and shamed them, calling on them to surrender for investigation, furthermore he ordered security personnel to be withdrawn from the military officers and politicians he had mentioned in his speech. As is clear from the rhetoric the national police and judiciary were then mobilised in a strategy that seeks to criminalise and punish rather than rehabilitate users and mitigate demand, as favoured by many Europeans states.

The police operations, which were implemented within the first month of his reign, consisted of door to door searches on a massive scale, targeting not only the drug dealers and their suppliers, but also known drug addicts. In fact, Duterte does not distinguish between addicts and dealers claiming, they are one and the same, as drug users will invariably deal in order to keep their own habits going. Given the horizontal nature of drug distribution in the nation, there is some logic to this argument. According to the Filipino online news portal Rappler by mid-February 2020 there had been a total of 153,851 anti-drug operations, 223,780 drug personalities arrested, and 14 clandestine laboratories dismantled. Alone in the first six months of his incumbency the police had carried out operations covering 5.6 million homes. In terms of deaths however there remains a great disparity between the statistics being presented by the state and those presented by human rights groups. With 5,563 and over 27000 deaths being reported respectively (Rappler 2016). Given the highly politicised nature of the Philippine war on drugs it is perhaps reasonable to conclude that both reports may be dubious. In a re-evaluation of their statistics the Police have removed "homicide cases under investigation" fearing that the figures were being mangled together with deaths linked to police operations. In this category there are around 30,000 cases outstanding and it is here we enter a grey area. Then one of the major accusations labelled against the government is that they are partaking in the extra judicial killing of suspects then shifting the blame onto vigilantes. In an expose for Reuters two Filipino officers who have released a paper entitled "The state-sponsored extrajudicial killings in the Philippines" seem to confirm this argument and they are not alone in doing so. In their report it's authors describe how murders are arranged in order to obtain cash rewards for removing drug related personalities. It documents how civilians from the Davao Death squad are being deployed in order to "augment and assist" the anti-drugs campaign.

Reuters however appear cautious with their report, noting that the paper they were presented with, offers only "granular" evidence, while hinting that its release could be politically motivated. As the article notes "the second half of the report is largely political in nature, asserting that Duterte has close ties to Communist forces in the Philippines. Many in the military and police are concerned by what they see as Duterte's leftist sympathies" Given the earlier removals of high-ranking officials within the state apparatus it is clear to see why some feel antipathy towards Duterte (Reuters Apr 2017). Yet these accusations are not new and are echoed among religious and human rights groups across the country, finding consensus worldwide. As for Duterte himself? Well his savage words alone may easily be construed as self-incriminating. The reports link to the Davao Death Squad is particularly significant in as much as Duterte was mayor of Davao prior to his appointment as president.

In early spring 2017 Arturo Lascanas a former police officer gave explosive testimony at the Philippine senate. He described how he had taken part in extra-judicial killings in Davao during Duterte's tenure as mayor, in particular his deposition linked the president to the death squad. Lascanas is on record elsewhere talking about the tens of thousands of pesos he earned per operation in the early 2000s (Reuters Apr 2017). Either way it is beyond reproach that the Philippines has an incredibly high death rate in "legitimate anti-drug operations". Equally drug related murders by international comparisons remain incredibly high, realities therefore that tell their own story. We can assume that if no link does exist between state security apparatus and vigilantes, then the Duterte government at the very least has managed to generate an environment highly conducive for the murder of those associated with narcotics. Then the combination of offering immunity to police involved in the killings, the bounties rewarded, not to mention the dehumanising language used are long thought to prime countries for mass atrocities. It is on this basis that some such as Maia Szalavitz writing in the Washington Post have come to label the Philippines drug war as a genocide, here the outer group simply comprises drug addicts rather than an ethnic minority (Szalavitz 2016). Undoubtedly there are some traits in the killings that are identifiable with the innate processes that may unfold into such crimes against humanity. For example, in their work on the Rwandan genocide Hoax and Smeulers identify certain dynamics which facilitated the mass murders. For example they point to crimes of obedience, where lower ranking officials carry out a killing because they feel entitled to do so by the authorities, given an air of legitimacy others may feel they are operating in a legal vacuum where they can exact revenge and settle scores without getting caught. Such opportunistic crimes are known to rise in an environment of real or perceived immunity. In the case of the Philippines the use of excessive force has not only been condoned and justified but considered a duty. Consummate with the work of Hoax and Smeulers we can deduct that Duterte openly calling for drug personalities to be killed, added to the conforming and consensus mechanisms within a hierarchical institution such as the police can cause the breakdown of norms that otherwise inhibit extreme violence. Primarily this is due to de-individuated behaviour where perpetrators feel less accountable and subsequently less restrained. All this backed up by the language of war (Smeulers & Hoax 2010). This language was clearly on display even during Duterte's reign as major of Davao, where he had warned that criminals were a "legitimate target of assassination". With human rights watch noting that some victims had been killed after Duterte had announced their names in a television broadcast. He is also on record as supporting the death squads (Guardian Aug 2016). As such even killer groups such as the infamous Davao Death squad could operate without having to fear reprisals from the national authorities. On the contrary they received accolades. In addition further dynamics are identifiable with the local mind set orientated on patronage, then the new recruits who had replaced the previous officers and high ranking officials were at times directly dependent on the president for their new found positions, the resultant kinetics of this reality are the invisible bonds of loyalty which connect the police etc to Duterte on a somewhat personal level psychologically.

Irrespective of international condemnation the president continues to enjoy high levels of public support, much to the chagrin of rights groups. This support even reached new highs in January 2020 when Duterte was polling at +72 (Bloomberg Jan2020).

According to Lasco for many of the country's citizens the killings are seen "as a necessary evil to get rid of the far worse menace of drug addicts and the criminality associated with them". Many attest to the fact that Duterte transformed Davao from one of the most dangerous cities in Asia into one of its safest (Lasco 2017).

So, what do we find in the way of alternatives to the Philippines bloody war on drugs? Are there viable options given the countries unfavourable topography and societal strains in seeking remedies? This is quintessential to our enquiry then the Philippines has arrived at this juncture not by chance. Due to the countries poor infrastructure the Philippines has long been reliant on its international partners to help them devise strategies with which to fight organised crime. By the end of July 2016 Obama had pledged $32 million dollars to help the Philippines in combating crime, China too plays a prominent role in supporting the state authorities. US aid is issued in order to promote justice sector reforms, enhance police training and in general work towards reducing drug demand. Further the US coast guard is working to build a Philippines coast guard capable not only of interdicting transnational shipments of drugs, but also to make them a capable force in fighting crime in general.

While the intentions are laudable, it remains unrealistic to expect such measures to have a deep impact. This is put into perspective by acknowledging that the USA itself is unable to successfully secure its own more delineated borders. Securing those of the Asian nations incredibly fragmented land mass with infinitely less resources, would appear to render the US aid as little more than a show of good faith. The same could be said of its reforms in the criminal justice system, where its constituents are the benefactors of the "Padrino system". By funding and creating a network of local NGOs a strategy of soft power has been devolved by which good governance and accepted standards of practice are to be encouraged, yet nepotism and patronage are endemic and reflect the general moral malaise that has befallen the country. The corruption and human rights abuses therefore form what currently appear to be an indelible and symbiotic relationship (Hembra 2004) (US deprt state).

Yet the killing of thousands of "drug personalities" seems to be some form of logic fallacy. Then are we really claiming that the criminal problem is solved by committing what is regarded morally as one of humanity's most heinous and abominable acts, namely, to kill? Especially where consequential outcomes cannot be assured. Again, the perception of the drug deaths is seemingly skewed by some of the very dynamics that help perpetuate the killings in practice. As addressed earlier these dynamics are top down legitimisation, dehumanisation of a potentially dangerous other and the de-individuation of the perceiver. Public perception therefore has been framed, which in turn has blurred and diminished moral indignation of the killings that under any other circumstances would be viewed with horror (Smeulers & Hoax 2010).

Is there a clear solution?

Lascos believes a solution could be found in education. People should be given a deeper understanding about drug use, he associates misinformation with the general public's acquiescence to the government's stance, academics and journalists he posits should be charged with enlightening the public. Lascos also suggests that the narcotics situation by Asian standards could be comparatively low, while acknowledging that a true picture given the unreliability of the statistics is hard to come by. By making people conscious of the fact that the country has a correlatively lower drug rate than its neighbours it is hoped that the killings will be viewed as illegitimate. That drug use is currently low on the other hand is cogent given the mass incarcerations and the killings, such a rationalisation therefore may only serve the current course (Lasco 2017). In 2017 a non-profit network comprising 50 universities and 167 participants from 10 mostly East-Asian states entitled "the Global Health Program of the Association of the Pacific Rim Universities" held a conference in Manila on the question of the Philippines narcotics problem. Their aim was to push current trends towards a more human rights and public health orientated policy. They devised what became known as the Manila declaration, a set of suggestions which implores the Philippine government to execute:

"drug control policies and strategies that incorporate evidence-based, socially acceptable, cost-effective, and rights-based approaches that are designed to minimize, if not to eliminate, the adverse health, psychological, social, economic and criminal justice consequences of drug abuse towards the goal of attaining a society that is free from crime and drug and substance abuse;

Recognizing, further, that drug dependency and co-dependency, as consequences of drug abuse, are mental and behavioral health problems, and that in some areas in the Philippines injecting drug use comorbidities such as the spread of HIV and AIDS are also apparent, and that current prevention and treatment interventions are not quite adequate to prevent mental disorders, HIV/AIDS and other co-morbid diseases among people who use drugs;

Affirming that the primacy of the sanctity/value of human life and the value of human dignity, social protection of the victims of drug abuse and illegal drugs trade must be our primary concern;

And that all health, psycho-social, socio-economic and rights-related interventions leading to the reduction or elimination of the adverse health, economic and social consequences of drug abuse and other related co-morbidities such as HIV/AIDS should be considered in all plans and actions toward the control, prevention and treatment of drug and substance abuse;

As a community of health professionals, experts, academics, researchers, students and health advocates, we call on the Philippine government to address the root causes of the illegal drug problem in the Philippines utilizing the aforementioned affirmations. We assert that the drug problem in the country is but a symptom of deeper structural ills rooted in social inequality and injustice, lack of economic and social opportunities, and powerlessness among the Filipino people. Genuine solutions to the drug problem will only be realized with the fulfillment and enjoyment of human rights, allowing them to live in dignity deserving of human beings. As members of educational, scientific and health institutions of the country, being rich and valuable sources of human, material and technological resources, we affirm our commitment to contribute to solving this social ill that the Philippine government has considered to be a major obstacle in the attainment of national development." (Global Health 2017)

The declarations aim's are honourable, but are they realistic? Certainly, change cannot happen overnight. Some of the declarations require fundamental changes in the socio-political and economic superstructure of the state. In the Philippines as we have examined elsewhere there has been a negative social impact generated from the high levels of inequality and the subsequent injustices these have provoked. Yet genuine change in a developing state such as the Philippines is perhaps more complex than in the first world, then exogenous pressures and demands such as structural adjustments from the institutions of global governance can restrict not only democracy, but policy as a whole. It is against this background that the Manila declaration in some sense looks more utopian than practical. A lot of its key ideas appear to be a reiteration of points made the year before in the International Narcotics Control Boards annual report, where it stated that the international drug treaties do not "mandate a war on drugs". The INCB also promoted policies that sought to ensure the health and wellbeing of the worlds citizens. Yet there are no signs of change emanating from Manila that current policy is to be reviewed (UNODC IRI 2016). Could mobilising the international community on the other hand induce Duterte to take a more humane approach? In July 2019 the international community upped the ante when a UN resolution put forward by Iceland at the human rights council was accepted. There will now follow an investigation into the mass killings.

Unsurprisingly Duterte has not been cowed, once more the perennial weakness in the UNs "consensual" and rather toothless nature are exposed, "I will never allow myself to answer these whites" he proclaimed whilst addressing military personnel."I will never, never, never answer any question coming from you"

In a further tirade Duterte sought to discredit what he deems a Western vision of rights when bellowing "your concern is human rights, mine is human lives" Running concurrently with the UN investigation is a crimes against humanity inquiry by the International Criminal Court in the Hague. For the ICC crimes against humanity are "serious violations committed as part of a large-scale attack against any civilian population" (Guardian Feb 2018).

In toe with their definition the court had received a report laying out evidence that Duterte was directly linked to extra-judicial killings as far back as 1988 and throughout his time as mayor of Davao city. Yet the rump of the investigation appears to be from 2016 onwards as Fatou Bensouda explained when saying that her office would be "analysing crimes allegedly committed ... since at least 1 July 2016 in the context of the 'war on drugs' campaign" Duterte responded in his usual defiant manner by unilaterally withdrawing his country's membership of the court, with the justification that the inquiry was of a political nature and that it had denied him a presumption of innocence. Nonetheless the Philippines departure does little to protect him in strict legal terms, as the ICC prosecutor explained "jurisdiction applies to crimes committed while a country is a member". Nonetheless problems with the case are unfolding, dampening the initial joy and hope the inquiry had given civil society groups. An attorney Jude Sabio representing a key witness as part of the ongoing investigation stated that the ICC case was being used as a "tool for propaganda" by the local opposition to Duterte and that it should be set aside. Sabio has since withdrawn his testimony at the ICC. Any ulterior motive behind this sudden about turn have not yet been identified, no doubt suspicions abound (Reuters Jan 2020)

The ICC has some way to go before it can becoming a genuine Leviathan, some hope is placed in the soft power dynamics the court can exert. We assume that Duterte could find himself in hot water should he be voted out of government in the future and therefore might seek to curb the violence he is accused of unleashing. Until that happens there is a long way to go. As stated earlier he enjoys very high levels of support not only popular, but among the legislative too. Crime rates in the Philippines are down 20%, drug use on the streets is lower. If education is the answer as Lasco suggests, then challenging Duterte's popularity alone could be a hurdle to high, otherwise the best-case scenario would mean waiting patiently for a generational change in the country before the fruits of such social engineering could be seen (Reuters Dec 2019).

And yet it is wholly intolerable that the procedures of due process be discarded. This is a fundamental right, which even the most regressive voices in the natural rights theories acknowledge (Tuck 1979). Additionally, solving the self-inflicted damage that addicts bring on themselves by misusing drugs with mortal violence is a highly perplexing concept, especially in terms of social ills caused. The deaths resonate of course far beyond the immediate person being killed. In fact, the killings look like a superficial remedy that fails to grapple with the social conditions that help foster drug use. It is after all apparent that the social strains and inequalities that rage in the Philippines, are conducive to a prevalent narcotics scene. Such understandings should provide a more empathetic approach and echo Lascos stance mentioned above. Again, we agree that drug users should be aided in kicking their habits, but such idealism seems constrained by time and time is vital, then Duterte's methods are attracting praise in other Asian states, with authorities in Sri Lanka, Bangladesh and Indonesia toying with his model (Global Health 2019). It is clear that there are no easy and immediate solutions, certainly states all around the world need to create greater social equilibrium. States must also honour the terms of their social contracts and move in unison to redress the imbalances. Does killing one's citizens fit into the latter?

Chapter 15

Global policing and legal frameworks for combating drug trafficking

In chapter one we examined how the prohibition of drugs came to be viewed internationally as the legitimate means by which nations approach bot the subject of psychoactive drug consumption and the illicit markets that cater for them, we also concluded that the war on drugs had by and large not achieved its objectives, despite some claims to the contrary. In chapter two we looked at the effects of globalization in the development of the illicit worldwide narco-market. We found that the neoliberal deregulation of global markets that were promoted during the mid-1980s added to by a withering away of the nation states external boundaries, plus the advancement in new transport networks were bringing the world and therefore the sources of illicit drug production and their prospective markets closer together.

We also looked at both sociological and criminological perspectives on global anomie and the way in which consumerist cultural goals were being conveyed via global media platforms. A strong correlation between the deterritorialization of culture and the insecurities born of new reference points of mass consumption to which many across the globe have no legitimate access were recognized. The social strains sharpened by what Passas calls global anomie is likely to create a criminogenic contagion especially in weak or failed states as well as among communities excluded by economic and social mobility within the "first world". In short globalization is both expounding criminal tendencies and providing easier access to illegitimate markets.

This chapter therefore looks at what can be done to address a forecast that predicts an extension of the global drugs market. The answer for many is to be found in a form of global policing (Aas 2007)(Bowling & Sheptycki 2012) (Naim 2005). Global policing has come to the fore with the realization that drug traffickers have largely succeeded in exploiting the legal and policing gaps in a system intrinsically transnational in nature but stubbornly Westphalian jurisprudentially. The rapid change in the dynamics of the world's now interdependent structure has led to the formulation of an extremely cogent realization: A need to catch the globetrotting bad guy, calls for a global police force. Be that as it may the creation of such a body remains improbable given the innate suspicions and complexities of the international relations arena, a realm ardently beholden to the concept of the nation state and a continued desire by their actors not to relinquish power (Bowling & Sheptycki 2012). Further the potential for legal, cultural and even religious discrepancies arising out of the Inquisitive, Adversarial, Sharia and Communist competing legal systems is another issue to be addressed. As is jurisdiction and accountability, after all there is no global social contract upon which a global police force may stake its legitimacy (Dammer et al 2014). As a consequence, Bowling and Sheptycki promote the emergence instead of what they refer to as global policing. A network of police technocrats whose mission is entirely toothless, but whose mandate is dominated by the dissemination of intelligence across national boundaries, coercion therefore remaining the prerogative of the state (Bowling & Sheptycki 2012). This idea of global policing is based on a transnational structure of policing agents and organizations such as the UN with all its principal organs, subsidiaries and associates. Other major players include the FATF an International Governmental Organization (IGO) charged with policing the global money system, Interpol a 188-member strong policing institution whose primary role is to gather and disseminate intelligence. Interpol acts as a communications hub for transnational policing via its National Central Bureaux, then there is the World's Customs Organization and the police unit of the international Criminal Court Police not to mention a whole plethora of other organizations who share in the worldwide policing architecture (Bowling & Sheptycki 2012). The most prominent of these organizations given its universal membership is without doubt the UN. It has created an impressive set of treaties and conventions that have attempted to unify international policy with regards to drug trafficking. The most important documents that reflect these endeavours are "the single convention on narcotic drugs", amended in 1972 by the "1971 Convention on Psychotropic Substances" and the "United Nations Convention against Illicit Traffic in Narcotic Drugs and Psychotropic Substances of 1988" (UNODC Online). The latter conventions key paragraph is Article three which calls for the criminalization of all those involved in the drug business from cultivation to distribution.

Article 3. Offences and sanctions 1. Each Party shall adopt such measures as may be necessary to establish as criminal offences under its domestic law, when committed intentionally: (a) (i) The production, manufacture, extraction; preparation, offering, offering for sale, distribution, sale, delivery on any terms whatsoever, brokerage, dispatch, dispatch in transit, transport, importation or exportation of any narcotic drug or any psychotropic substance contrary to the provisions of the 1961 Convention, the 1961 Convention as amended or the 1971 Convention; (UN 1988)

The convention then asks nations to adopt the following set of provisions on those found guilty/accused of Article three.

(Please turn page)

A. The confiscation of the process or assets obtained by the means of article three paragraph 1.
B. The extradition of anyone found guilty or suspected of any of the conditions laid out in article 3 paragraph 1
C. That mutual legal assistance shall be offered between parties in relation to any one being investigated under article 13 paragraph 1
D. That a transfer of proceedings may occur in the interests of a fair trial for those suspected of any act under the provisions of article 3 paragraph 1 (UN 1988)

In spite of the undoubted effort and hope given to these instruments and other treaties, conventions etc. Their implementation is not readily achievable. Indeed, the conventions on closer inspection generally include an array of clauses that can be employed to refuse grounds for any call for cooperation. This may chiefly be the result of a conflict between domestic law and the requirements of the international treaties/conventions etc. Extradition treaties as an example are generally conditioned by the rule of double criminality (The offence must be recognized in both the requesting and requested state) in order for one nation to hand over a suspect to another (Joutsen 2014). Further many nations refuse in accordance with domestic law to hand over their citizens to a requesting state (Joutsen 2014). Other grounds for refusing cooperation may be brought forth on the grounds that assistance could pose a threat to sovereignty, security, law, order or some other vital interest (Joutsen 2014)or simply the assistance being required does not fall in line with legal procedures of the state being requested (Joutsen 2104). The above four provisions which call for cooperation, nonetheless, fall within the scope of Article 2 paragraphs 2 and 3 that affirm the none interference or violation of other states sovereignty (UN 1988). A law often viewed as an unnecessary restriction on powerful states who seek to eradicate drugs at their source (Naim 2005)(Woodwiss 2003).

But beyond simple technicalities the global policing architecture is inefficient by its perceived inequalities. As Bowling and Sheptycki explain there is an innate "western bias" situated at the core of this global policing, in which policy is being driven by the over-developed world that comprises the seigneurial states whose "interests tend to dominate political institutions of the world system (Bowling & Sheptycki 2012). An example of such predilection is encapsulated by the way in which Interpol has been "successively captured by different states interests" starting in 1923 when it was effectively an arm of the Austrian state police, the second world war saw it fall into the hands of the Nazis, which then made way for French domination after Germanys defeat in 1945(Bowling & Sheptycki 2012). Currently it appears to be under the auspices of the United States who made flagrant use of its apparent neutral organizational stance in order to expand their policing capabilities deep into the Caribbean (Bowling & Sheptycki 2012). Naturally suspicions are constructed elsewhere in the world in response to these blatant discrepancies(Naim 2005), leading to a fragmentation of global governance in regard to security and issues of criminality, hence the development of regional police bodies such as Europol (Naim 2005) and ASEANPOL whose names infer their area of operation. These organizations are culturally more homogenous than a universal body such as Interpol where definitions of crimes are almost impossible to define. (Terrorism being an example. Hamas and Hezbollah are not recognized as terrorist organizations in many parts of the world) (Bowling & Sheptycki 2012).

Both ASEANPOL and Europol are based on Interpol like structures and work at the forefront of intelligence led policing. Such regional entities are more effective at establishing grundnorms in their area of operation (Naim 2005). Nonetheless cooperation can be fraught with difficulties, indeed this is the case even on a nation state level where turf wars between varying government agencies are well documented, and then there are the immense bureaucracies and the individual psyches at play all of which needs immense coordination. Individuals may peruse their own interests or those of their organizations. In this regard Naim highlights the lack of cooperation between the CIA and FBI that perhaps could have prevented 9/11 (Naim 2005), but the most obvious obstruction to success in fighting drugs is the reality that all the major sources of psychoactive substances are situated in areas of virtually no state control. It is highly unlikely that the Colombian government is in a position to comply with a request for extradition if a wanted trafficker is to be found in FARC controlled territory (Stares 1996). Similarly, we must be aware of the endemic corruption that those states associated with drug cultivation are beset by (Paoli et al 2009). So not only is global policing restricted by the interests of state sovereignty, but it is stymied by bureaucracy, legal differences, competing judicial systems, the desires of its individual actors, corruption, weak state control and a lack of presence in the areas that pose a definitive security threat (Bowling & Sheptycki 2012) (Naim 2005). This is not to say there are no success stories, however the continued failure of policing organizations to tackle the growing illicit drugs industry points to a need for a more radical solution than mere police partnerships (Jenner 2014). As a consequence, should alternative policies be considered?

Decriminalization

The policy of decriminalization is not to be confused with concepts of legalization. Decriminalization to all intents and purposes insists on punitive measures for drug dealing and trafficking in much the same way as prohibition, however users are not subjected to any form of sanction for the possession of a drug deemed to be for personal use (Inciardi 1999). The policy is one that rests on pragmatism. Those who support decriminalization point at the shortcomings of current policy, the failure to prevent youths from initiating with drug consumption and the burden that is placed, on the criminal justice system (Inciardi 1999). Further they recognize the health dangers subsumed in criminalization and seek to promote harm reduction to address the needs of substance abusers (Husak & De Marneffe 2005). However, the constant attack from those who prefer the illegality of drugs point to the dangers of decriminalization. They see decriminalization as condoning the use of drugs by removing the social barriers that would act as a deterrent, secondary to which is increased drug use (Inciardi 1999). A result not evident in Portugal, a country that has applied de facto decriminalization since 2001. As we see from the table overleaf. (Graham 2014)

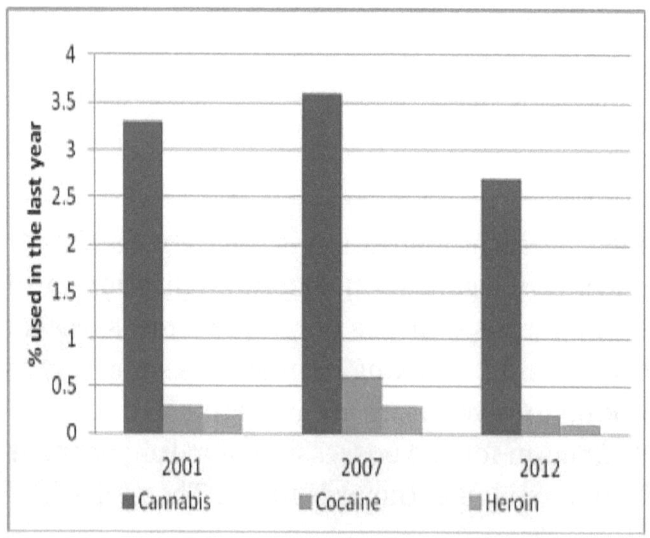

After an initial increase we see a longer-term reduction of drug consumption in all three categories, but it is in health care that the Portuguese policy has been an irrefutable success with drug related pathologies such as hepatitis, sexually transmitted diseases and drug overdoses being dramatically reduced (Graham 2014)

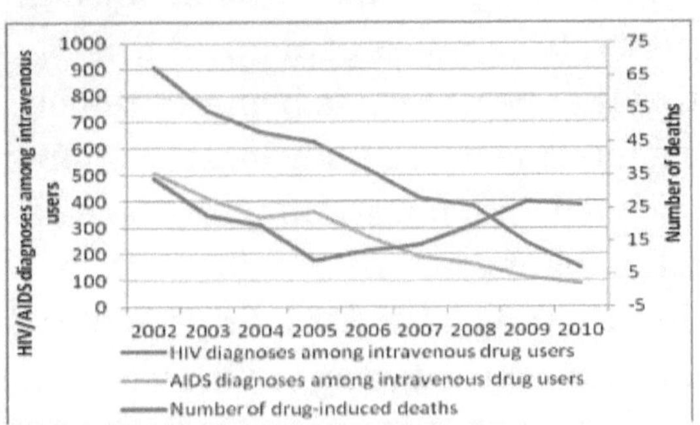

These are the result of Portugal introducing "safer injecting rooms" or "shooting galleries" as they are often referred to, they provide medical facilities in case of an overdose, clean syringes and access to counselling (Chambliss et al 2010). The results in Portugal are by no means unique. Switzerland while not implementing a policy of decriminalization, has similarly obtained noteworthy results by providing harm reduction facilities in which drug use is tolerated. Similarly, the Swiss government has introduced supervised injectable heroin (SIH), it is a policy whereby heroin is given by the state to entrenched drug users, in harm reduction facilities. Once again, we are dealing with a de facto decriminalization of drugs, even if it is area specific

(Chambliss et al 2010). The Swiss experience proved irrefutably successful, reducing the mortality rate to 1% compared with 8,9% for those who injected elsewhere, moreover drug deaths dropped dramatically from 419 in 1992 the year of its introduction to 159 in 1999 and remained stable at 1% until its final recording in 2005 what is more there was not a single death recorded amongst the programmes participants while injecting in a shooting gallery. (Chambliss et al 2010) It is worth mentioning that heroin while being extremely addictive is not damaging to the body in itself, more it is problems associated with uncertain purity levels that are the predominant cause of overdose, while HIV and hepatitis are transmitted via dirty needles. In addition, injecting can cause damage to the veins and lead to sores and infections, all of which may be ameliorated by harm reduction facilities (Nutt 2012). High purity heroin may also be smoked and provides an alternative to injecting, but it is prohibitive policies that seriously limit its availability (Nutt 2012). Despite the heady achievements that this policy has enjoyed in Switzerland it has been limited to well documented problem users who have repeatedly failed in other programmes such as methadone replacement schemes. This half-closed door policy allows criminal elements still to remain embedded in the Swiss illicit drugs market. The criminal element has been a particularly problematic issue in Mexico where decriminalization came into law in 2009. The Mexican example allowed possession of a limited amount of drugs, freeing the criminal justice system to concentrate its efforts on the major cartels, but despite some impressive arrests the drugs business continues to prosper, while drug related violence continues to increase unabated.(Janner 2014) An additional problem noted when drugs remain in the hands of criminals is the level of purity. Drug users can never be sure exactly how a substance has been cut; meaning overdose is a persistent risk (Nutt 2012).

Legalisation

A way to incorporate, the harm reduction policies associated with decriminalization and the removal of the violent and dangerous nature of the illicit drug market is legalization, however supporters generally concede that some form of regulation must take place, much in the way it does today with alcohol and tobacco, where age limits and licencing obligations are stipulated in law (Inciardi 1999). It is also advised that profit motivations be removed from the sale of drugs, after all the aim is not to promote their use via marketing campaigns, hence it should come under the auspices of government control rather than being pursuant to the free market (Kleiman et 2011). Legalization in its purest sense is antithetical to the dominant policy of criminalization (Kleiman et al 2011). What is more from a philosophical point of view it is closely linked to the libertarian cogitations of J.S.Mills, whose opus magnus On Liberty is often referred to by those who reject the paternalism inherent in prohibition (Husak & De Marneffe 2005). Mills in contrast to the constrained beliefs of Calvinism has repeatedly come to represent the empowerment of the individual to act and think freely, and that such liberty is essential to the development of mankind. Mills expresses the conviction that any "individual should not be deterred from carrying his opinions into practice at his own cost, that mankind are not infallible: that their truths, for the most part, are only half-truths: that unity of opinion, unless resulting from the fullest and freests comparison of opposite opinion, is not desirable and diversity not an evil but a good" (Mills 1869) (1). Indeed, in this sense the religious moralism upon which prohibition rests its foundations may essentially be deemed as none binding to an atheist or a follower of a non-orthodox faith. That conjecture or mere belief can subject an individual to castigation somehow seems antagonistic to the secular world we in the West live in, as it does to an individual's human right to diversity, hence the drug debate can simply be reduced to a question of personal morality. Consequentially any kind of paternalistic legislation should be considered void as no legislator is ever justified in believing that another mature adult is mistaken about what is best for themselves (Husak & De Marneffe 1989). Certainly, there is a philosophical element within the field of jurisprudence that rejects any form of legal moralism outright, sighting its basis for punishing individuals on superstition alone as invalid, however it is a theory that remains at the periphery. (Husak&De Marneffe 2005). Nonetheless as Husak points out, most people living today no longer concur with the belief "that an activity is immoral simply because it produces pleasure" (Husak &De Marneffe 2005) thus modern day tendencies it would seem are inimical to the Calvinist posture which contends "what is not duty is a sin" (Mills 1869). Moreover, if recreational pleasure is immoral, how must we deem drug consumption, in the light of the licit nature of tobacco and Alcohol, does it not stand to reason that their legality be repealed? This striking inconsistency remains a central feature upon which libertarians argue their case (Husak & De Marneffe 2005), as is the horrific health damage afflicted on users by banned substances due to their impurity and by a lack of health provisions, that are part and parcel of current stance (Kleiman et al 2005). However, sticking to the philosophical debate for the time being it is perhaps sub judice for the legalization camp to assert the support of Mills in their quest for an overhaul of current policy. Mills after all transmits in "On liberty" an insistence that others should not be damaged as a consequence of individual acts " of whatever kind, which, without justifiable cause, do harm to others, may be, and in the more important cases absolutely require to be controlled by the unfavourable sentiments, and, when needful, by the active interference of mankind. The liberty of the individual must be far limited; he must not make himself a nuisance to other people" (Mills 1869). Here Mills is clearly advocating social restrictions on behaviour detrimental to society, of which the use of drugs, especially in view of the criminal activities associated with addiction or the health effects that burden the social system could be implied (Inciardi 1999), but by the same token are the proscriptive measures to combat drugs more damaging and costly to the overall wellbeing of society? From the work covered above we must surely say yes, especially when considering a global perspective, but we must also contend that for the time being there is disparity in the distribution of harm done across the globe and until we find the first world being thrown into a Mexico type scenario there is little probability of change (Keefer & Loayza 2010). Nonetheless we must be certain that unless new technologies are forthcoming, more and more drugs will be found entering our markets, we may assume this is a process already underway, as is made clear by increased interdiction rates that are backed up by falling narcotic prices (UNODC 2015). This reality points to a failure of the drugs war, which equates to the success of criminal organized groups. Legalization under government control would mean an end to global criminalized drug networks and would guarantee quality control for domestic users. A contentious argument suggests that the legalization of drugs could even reduce overall crime rates (especially if harm reduction policies run concurrently), by introducing competition to challenge the dominance of alcohol with all its links to violent behaviour (Nutt 2012). This rational posits that the majority of those ingesting Amphetamines, Cannabis, Ketamine or Ecstasy are highly unlikely to be involved in the aggressive anti-social behaviour for which alcohol is notorious and which costs the UK taxpayer in the region of £6 billion a year (Nutt 2012). Further they could reap a small tax that could be pumped into anti-drug education and harm reduction facilities. Once more prohibitionists confront such arguments with talk of increased consumption, but de facto legalization of cannabis in the Netherlands has not been consistent with such a scenario, although consumption rates could greatly divulge depending on the substance being consumed (EMCDDA 2015). Equally we may claim, that legalization could reduce consumption even if acknowledging that in the short term an initial increase could occur. The social damage created by such an increase could invariably spark a reactionary movement against drug use in accordance with Durkheim's theories of social control mechanisms and bring rates down to new lows (Hayward & Morrison 2012). We may find evidence of such a correlation by looking at drug consumption in Portugal since the introduction of decriminalization where an initial increase was followed by a new low some ten years later (Graham 2014). Other historical accounts of prohibition, such as the criminalization of alcohol that began in The US in 1919 saw increased alcohol ingestion every year after 1921, signalling the insignificance of the policy. Where the intemperance movement appears to have left its biggest mark was in the years leading up to the implementation of the criminalization of alcohol and shows the power of socialization and the way in which a substance can be stigmatized (Thorington1996) (Clark 1976). It is not by accident that heroin, given its powerfully addictive qualities and its threat to health is consumed by a far smaller user base then cannabis (UNODC 2015).

Obstacles to legalization

Undoubtedly there are many hindrances to legalization, foremost appears to be public opinion which according to recent polls appears against the non-criminalization of drugs with perhaps the exception being cannabis (Guardian 2014)(Swanson 2013). This public opinion in a functioning democracy gives legitimacy to a policy even if a law is technically viewed as a negative contagion (Thomas 2008).

Public orientated legitimacy remains a categorical imperative even if public opinion has been manipulated by fear, fear which in the realm of drug use is associated to a fear of what Van Duyne calls the wrong state of mind, which has its basis in pharmacological Calvinism (Van Duyne & Levi 2005) an additional source of fear is the foreign other, the interplay between these two factors is where we find the historical context in which prohibition was formed. Since then a fear of drugs has been propagated by successive governments impacting on a common perception of illicit substances (Husak & De Marneffe 2005). As humans we appear afraid of the "other" believing in the recklessness of our fellow citizens in what correlates closely to the *illusion of superiority*, the well documented cognitive bias in which individuals overestimate their own qualities and abilities relative to others " I would not take heroin if it was legal tomorrow, but it's those others who would" from this state of mind apocalyptical scenarios with relation to drug legalization may be formed (Horswill, Waylen, Alexander & Mckenna 2004). While fear may be pernicious to an individual, it is also a tool by which governments and agencies seek legitimacy in politically motivated actions and serves to conceal a democratic deficit that is becoming increasingly apparent in the sphere of global governance/policing.(Woodwiss 2003)(Sheptycki 2003)(Sheptycki 1996)

Prohibition as such is therefore often key to foreign policy as Niam explains in his informative investigative work "Illicit". Countries that cooperate with US drug policy "receive military, technical, and financial support. Those that do not risk the consequences: public shaming, economic sanctions, or back-channel punitive uses of American influence with international funding agencies like the World Bank and IMF" (Naim 2005) While at the same time drugs may serve as tools to undermine foreign governments and aid funding for political insurgencies as such some may deduce that the prohibitive framework serves to cement a form of global governance conducive to hegemonic interests (McCoy 2003)(Glenny 2008)(Sheptycki2003).

Another obstacle is the realization that prohibition has become an industry in itself with outgoings of up to $100 Billion a year (Count the Cost 2012). To remove a network of organizations such as the DEA, ICE, the US Marshalls, the Air Smuggling Investigators Association, the Northern Working Group on the Suppression of Drug Trafficking and this is just organizations that are situated in the US (Naim 2005)(Bowling & Sheptychki 2012) let alone all the agencies that fight the drugs business all across the world, would lead to a loss of many jobs as well as influence. Moreover such organizations are notoriously hard to disassemble, (Naim 2005) as was noted in the case of NATO that had served its mandate once the cold war ended (Armstrong et al 2004).

Chapter 16

Conclusion & Recommendations

The legitimacy of a state is to be found in its social contract with its citizenry and in its classical triad of tasks to guarantee security, economic wellbeing and cultural identity (Baker 2003). It is in this realm that governments enact legislature in order to fulfil their obligations and it is against this background that the global policy of drug prohibition must be judged (Baker 2003), but the very nature of the social dynamics that have come to the fore in the last decades, dynamics associated with the process of globalization and neoliberalism have undermined many nation's abilities to address both the consumption of drugs and their trafficking (Baker 2003)(Lamy 2011). Indeed, globalization appears to have shifted the argument from one based on morality, public health and the well-being of the individual to one concerning peace and security (UNODC 2009). The inability of states to grapple with the issues central to what has become the universal "war on drugs" has created a law that to all intents and purposes has become a negative contagion (Jenner 2014) (Martin 2014). Indeed prohibition is primarily culpable of provoking a series of social pathogens such as corruption, the normalization of crime, murder and the proliferation of organized crime and terrorism both of whom share in the profits of an illicit industry valued at $500 billion a year (Count the Cost 2012)(Jenner 2014), furthermore these factors combine to attack already weak states at their core and embolden both criminal groups and insurgent groups yet further, thus the proverbial vicious circle is a direct consequence of current policy (Stares 1996).

To combat this global menace successive wars on drugs have been fought to which a transnational policing infrastructure has been added (McCoy 1972)(Sheptycki 1996), but due to the Hobbesian distrust inherent within the international political arena and questions of state sovereignty (Rittberger&Zangl 2006), not to mention the fact that most drug cultivating areas are actually operating in failed states beyond central government control (Kleiman et al 2009), the mission can only be described as an abject failure (Jenner 2014). What is more the continued globalization and the withering away of yet more borders added to the neoliberal economic policies that have dominated since the end of the cold war point to both increased supply and demand in the coming years, a fact related to the discernible feature of globalization that is the economic polarization of the north and the south (Stares 1996). With some commentators even going as far to suggest that globalization is creating wastelands or human waste in which the rich get richer and the poor get poorer (Baumann 2007), while media platforms such as the internet and satellite TV have become to the postmodern world, what print capitalism (2) became to the territorial state of the late 19th century, in that it has created an "imagined community" of shared values. Where print capitalism however had a unifying response within a countries borders, generally reinforcing concepts of national identity and culture, modern media is only highlighting the social and economic disparities idiosyncratic of our times (Aas 2007)(Linklater 2011). These disparities appear to be provoking forms of anomie and subsequently deviant behaviours (Passas 2000). In this book we examined these phenomena in post-communist Russia and the USA among others and presented various scenarios in which criminal elements have sought to exploit a lack of state control. In addition, we examined how ideas of cultural belonging added to by a shift in social reference points could expose fault lines in many nations in the years to come (Stares 1996) (Passas 2000).

Given the evidence throughout this essay and the cognisance that economic and migratory imperatives are only likely to facilitate a future increase in drug trafficking I suggest that the legalization of drugs be considered as a strategic option, given that current policy is seemingly unsustainable long term.

Government controlled legalization in conjunction with harm reduction facilities would give the authorities control over both the supply and demand aspect of the market. It would ensure clean substances, while controlling the source of supply, even determine where it comes from. It would be imperative to buy drugs at their source, enabling narcotics to be obtained at an incredibly reduced rate, hence completely pricing organized crime out of the market(Kleiman et al 2011)(Husak&De Marneffe 2005). By significantly reducing the profit margin transnational networks would collapse allowing the money invested in the war on drugs to be diverted into anti-drug education, health services and social services (UNODC 2014). Offering legitimate employment in source countries could create greater global stability too, by giving people something to hold onto, they ipso facto have something to lose. A factor of humanity not to be underestimated (Wilson 2008).

The drug debate we can say boils down to a balance of risk, risk between addiction and damage to individual health on one side and the risk of organized crime and now terrorism on the other (Inciardi 1999)(Kleiman et al 2011) (3). Risk is a part of life and is impossible to eradicate, we cannot account for the actions of every individual, but currently the war on drugs appears to be increasing harm not only to users but to society as a whole, further it can be seen to be threatening the very fabric of many nation states. If we try to predict the outcomes of legalization, then it is likely that a diversification of the drug market would reduce alcohol consumption and lead to an equivalent increase of miscellaneous drug use and thus unlikely to create the drug epidemic prohibitionists fear (Nutt 2012). It could be anticipated that designer drugs such as ecstasy would be consumed at a greater rate than they currently are. If this would be more dangerous to society than binge drinking is not apparent in the research conducted by Professor Nutt (2009). Problem drugs such as Crack and Heroin are usually consumed amongst certain disadvantaged or damaged sectors of society, thus a massive escalation would be unexpected (Wincup & Traynor 2009), but if we imagine a horror scenario in which say after ten years an epidemic has developed, then having destroyed most trafficking networks legalization could be repealed, with governments continuing to maintain addicts. This would prevent the re-establishment of criminal organizations re-entering the market as demand would be met by the authorities, leading to insufficient illicit demand from which organized gangs could profit (Van Duyne 2005). In forty years' time as addicts near the end of their lives we could be looking at a very different world in relation to drugs. I would suggest that perhaps a strategic move to legalization ceteris paribus is the only realistic step we can take to winning this war on drugs and yet risks remain. As the US experience has shown, even legally registered multinational motivated by profit can provoke a horrendous drugs epidemic. Therefore placing the state at the centre of such a radical policy becomes fundamental as does institutional oversight.

Nonetheless we acknowledge that currently such policies would be impossible to enact, drug legalisation remains a highly unpalatable concept and would require intense social engineering and a generational change before it could be considered a viable option. Not only this but such a move would require a concerted and united global effort among a large portion of the worlds nation states to be effective.

It is worth noting that the anomie provoked by globalisation and its integral neoliberal economic underpinnings have contributed indubitably to greater demand for narcotics. Greater distribution of wealth not to mention a more Keynesian approach to economics, one where the state acts as a pivotal arbiter between the interests of capital and labour and one where capital control, import substitution, subsides and some levels of protectionism would allow for greater economic growth and stability in the developing world, stability that invariably would help redress the imbalances especially where states are at their most vulnerable. Clearly such policies would be a good starting point for reducing the push and pull factors associated with the narcotics business and yet such a logical approach seems more unlikely then the fully blown drug legalisation mentioned above, however the aim here is surely to treat the social pathology with the relevant social intervention. Both the medicinal and social iatrogenic's associated with the illicit drug trade can be diminished, all the state has to do is take control.

Notes

(1) Freests: Appears to be a typing error, but is taken directly from Mills quote.

(2) Print Capitalism is the theory where by literature and print in general helped create a common language and sense of community within a given state. This sense of community proved to be the basis on which, according to some the modern state was formed.

(3) This is perhaps an over simplification and all arguments are still relevant, however it does appear that globalization and questions of security have now shifted the traditional drug debate, superseding previous arguments.

References

Without all the great work by the academics and professionals in this section my book would not have been possible. I owe a debt of gratitude to all of you.

Abadinsky, H. *Organized Crime* 7th Edition. Thomson Wadsworth, Belmont CA 2003. Pages 65-66

Abadinsky, H. *Organized Crime* 7th Edition. Thomson Wadsworth, Belmont CA 2003. Pages 64-66

Abadinsky, H. *Organized Crime* 7th Edition. Thomson Wadsworth, Belmont CA 2003. Pages 64-66

Abadinsky, H. *Organized Crime* 7th Edition. Thomson Wadsworth, Belmont CA 2003. Pages 69

Abadinsky, H. *Organized Crime* 7th Edition. Thomson Wadsworth, Belmont CA 2003. Pages 39 & 40

Aas, K F. *Globalization and Crime.* Routledge, London 2007. Pages 5, 47, 120-121, 173,207 & 208

Aas, K F. *Globalization and Crime.* Routledge, London 2007. Pages 90-93

Aas, K F. *Globalization and Crime.* Routledge, London 2007. Pages 8

Aas, K F. *Globalization and Crime.* Routledge, London 2007. Pages 90 & 102

Aas, K F. *Globalization and Crime*. Routledge, London 2007. Pages 92

Aas, K F. *Globalization and Crime*. Routledge, London 2007. Pages 120-122

Aas, K F. *Globalization and Crime*. Routledge, London 2007. Pages 120-122

Aas, K F. *Globalization and Crime*. Routledge, London 2007. Pages 120-134

Aas, K F. *Globalization and Crime*. Routledge, London 2007. Pages 19

Adams http://www.mirror.co.uk/news/uk-news/ipswich-superman-ecstasy-deaths-3-4910969

AECOM. http://www.aecom.com/Where+We+Are/Asia/Government/_carousel/Alternative+Development+Project+for+Northeast+Afghanistan

Al jaffal, O. https://asiatimes.com/2019/02/after-isis-iraq-has-a-drug-problem/ 2019

Ames.P *ISDS: The most toxic acronym in Europe.* Politico 17/09/2015

AP 2019. https://apnews.com/c428bb2ba4cd4cc6a59f8dbe79e18d9f

AP, Galofaro. 2019. https://news.yahoo.com/sackler-owned-opioid-maker-goes-053807260.html

The Atlantic 2019
https://www.theatlantic.com/international/archive/2019/08/philippines-dead-rodrigo-duterte-drug-war/595978/

Armstrong et al. *International Organization in World Politics*: Third Edition. Palgrave MacMillan. London 2004. Page 7

Baker, E. *The Legal Regulation of Organized Crime: Opportunities and Limitations. In Transnational Organized Crime.* Perspectives on Global Security. Edwards, A & Gill, P. Routledge, London 2003.Page 185

Baker, E. *The Legal Regulation of Organized Crime: Opportunities and Limitations. In Transnational Organized Crime.* Perspectives on Global Security. Edwards, A & Gill, P. Routledge, London 2003.Page 185-189

Baker, E. *The Legal Regulation of Organized Crime: Opportunities and Limitations. In Transnational Organized Crime.* Perspectives on Global Security. Edwards, A & Gill, P. Routledge, London 2003.Page 185-189

Baumann. In *Globalization and Crime.* Ed, Aas, K F. Sage, London 2007. Page 11

Baumann, M H. Published:⌐01 December 2017 Novel Synthetic Opioids andOverdose Deaths: Tip of the Iceberg?

Baylis,J et al. *The Globalization of World Politics*: An Introduction to International Relations. Oxford, Oxford 2011. Page 11

Baylis,J et al. *The Globalization of World Politics*: An Introduction to International Relations. Oxford, Oxford 2011. Page 535-536

Baylis,J et al. *The Globalization of World Politics*: An Introduction to International Relations. Oxford, Oxford 2011. Page 41-42

Baylis,J et al. *The Globalization of World Politics*: An Introduction to International Relations. Oxford, Oxford 2011. Page 369-372

BBC 2014. http://www.bbc.co.uk/news/uk-27235470

BBC 2019 *"On the Presidents orders"* Storyville.

BBC 2013. http://www.bbc.co.uk/news/world-europe-13194723

Behr, E. *Prohibition the 13 years that changed America*. BBC books, London 1997. Page 15-16

Bewley-Taylor. *United States and International Drug Policy 1909-1997*. Continuum, New York 2001. Pages 211-212

Blakeley, G 2019. Stolen, How to Save the World from Financialisation. Repeater. London. Pages 74-75

Blakeley, G 2019. Stolen, How to Save the World from Financialisation. Repeater. London. Pages 76-77

Blakeley, G 2019. Stolen, How to Save the World from Financialisation. Repeater. London. Pages 136-137

Bloomberg 2020
https://www.bloomberg.com/news/articles/2020-01-29/health-records-company-pushed-opioids-to-doctors-in-secret-deal

Bloomberg Jan 2020
https://www.bloomberg.com/news/articles/2020-01-22/duterte-s-popularity-hits-new-high-pollster-sws-says

Bowling, B & Sheptycki, J. *Global Policing*. Sage, London. 2012, Pages 29-52

Bowling, B & Sheptycki, J. *Global Policing*. Sage, London. 2012, Pages 29-52

Bowling, B & Sheptycki, J. *Global Policing*. Sage, London. 2012, Pages 53-77

Bowling, B & Sheptycki, J. *Global Policing*. Sage, London. 2012, Pages 52-77

Bowling, B & Sheptycki, J. *Global Policing*. Sage, London. 2012, Pages 6

Bowling, B & Sheptycki, J. *Global Policing*. Sage, London. 2012, Pages 55

Bowling, B & Sheptycki, J. *Global Policing*. Sage, London. 2012, Pages 56

Bowling, B & Sheptycki, J. *Global Policing*. Sage, London. 2012, Pages 68

Bowling, B & Sheptycki, J. *Global Policing*. Sage, London. 2012, Pages 101&102

Bowling, B & Sheptycki, J. *Global Policing*. Sage, London. 2012, Pages 65

Brown, S K & Bean, F D. *Assimilation Models, Old and New: Explaining Long and Short Term Process*. Migration Policy Institute. 2006

Brown, S K & Bean, F D. *Assimilation Models, Old and New: Explaining Long and Short Term Process*. Migration Policy Institute. 2006

Callimachi & Tondo. The Irish times https://www.irishtimes.com/news/world/middle-east/how-europe-s-drug-trade-scaled-up-straight-through-isis-turf-1.2790996 2016

Cardozo et al. 23 Febuary 2009. The Wall Street Journal. The war on drugs is a failure

Case & Deaton. *Deaths of despair and the future of capitalism*. Princeton 2020. Page 116

Case & Deaton. *Deaths of despair and the future of capitalism.* Princeton 2020. Page 1-15

Case & Deaton. *Deaths of despair and the future of capitalism.* Princeton 2020. Page 123

Case & Deaton. *Deaths of despair and the future of capitalism.* Princeton 2020. Page 259

Case & Deaton. *Deaths of despair and the future of capitalism.* Princeton 2020. Page 139

Case & Deaton. *Deaths of despair and the future of capitalism.* Princeton 2020. Page 150

Case & Deaton. *Deaths of despair and the future of capitalism.* Princeton 2020. Page 165

Case & Deaton. *Deaths of despair and the future of capitalism.* Princeton 2020. Page 147

Case & Deaton. *Deaths of despair and the future of capitalism.* Princeton 2020. Page 213

Case & Deaton. *Deaths of despair and the future of capitalism.* Princeton 2020. Page 225

Case & Deaton. *Deaths of despair and the future of capitalism.* Princeton 2020. Page 261

Case & Deaton. *Deaths of despair and the future of capitalism.* Princeton 2020. Page 248

CBS 2018 https://www.cbsnews.com/news/meet-60-minutes-dea-whistleblower/

CDC 2012
https://www.cdc.gov/mmwr/preview/mmwrhtml/mm6101a3.htm

Chambliss et al. *State Crime in a Global Age*. Willian Publishing, Cullompton Devon 2010. Pages 199-214

Chambliss et al. *State Crime in a Global Age*. Willian Publishing, Cullompton Devon 2010. Pages 201

Chambliss et al. *State Crime in a Global Age*. Willian Publishing, Cullompton Devon 2010. Pages 208

Chambliss et al. *State Crime in a Global Age*. Willian Publishing, Cullompton Devon 2010. Pages 203-205

Chambliss et al. *State Crime in a Global Age*. Willian Publishing, Cullompton Devon 2010. Pages 203-204

Christensen, J B. *Drugs, Deviancy and Democracy in Iran*: The Interaction of State and Civil Society.I.B Taurus 2011. Page 122

Christensen, J B. *Drugs, Deviancy and Democracy in Iran*: The Interaction of State and Civil Society.I.B Taurus 2011. Page 122

Clark, H N. *Deliver Us From Evil*: An Interpretation of American Prohibition. Norton New York 1976. Page 14

Clark, H N. *Deliver Us From Evil: An Interpretation of American Prohibition*. Norton New York 1976. Page 20

Clark, H N. *Deliver Us From Evil: An Interpretation of American Prohibition*. Norton New York 1976. Page 47

Clarke, C P. *ISIS is so desperate its turning to the drugs trade*. Rand Organisation https://www.rand.org/blog/2017/07/isis-is-so-desperate-its-turning-to-the-drug-trade.html 2019

Clegg & Branson. Guardian 3 March 2015. We have been losing the war on drugs for four decades end it now

Cloward, R A & Ohlin, L E. *Delinquency and Opportunity*. New York Free Press. New York 1960

Congress.gov 2016 https://www.congress.gov/bill/114th-congress/senate-bill/483/text

Corporate Europe Observatory 2019 https://corporateeurope.org/en/2019/05/high-prices-poor-access-eu-medicines-market-and-big-pharma

Count the Costs. Alternative drug 2012 report.https://www.unodc.org/documents/ungass2016//Contributions/Civil/Count-the-Costs-Initiative/AWDR.pdf Page 76

Count the Costs. Alternative drug 2012 report.https://www.unodc.org/documents/ungass2016//Contributions/Civil/Count-the-Costs-Initiative/AWDR.pdf Page 53

Count the Costs. Alternative drug 2012 report.https://www.unodc.org/documents/ungass2016//Contributions/Civil/Count-the-Costs-Initiative/AWDR.pdf Page 63&64

Count the Costs. Alternative drug 2012 report.https://www.unodc.org/documents/ungass2016//Contributions/Civil/Count-the-Costs-Initiative/AWDR.pdf Page 63&64

Count the Cost. Alternative Drug Report 2012https://www.unodc.org/documents/ungass2016//Contributions/Civil/Count-the-Costs-Initiative/AWDR.pdf. Page 8

Count the Cost. Alternative Drug Report 2012https://www.unodc.org/documents/ungass2016//Contributions/Civil/Count-the-Costs-Initiative/AWDR.pdf. Page 9

Dafflon, D. *Youth in Russia: The Portrait of a Generation in Transition.* Swiss Academy for Development. Biel 2009. Page 40

Daily Mail, June 2015. http://www.dailymail.co.uk/sciencetech/article-2624237/How-rap-reveals-trends-DRUGS-Graphs-hip-hop-lyrics-plot-rise-fall-illegal-substances.html

Desilver, D. *For most US workers, real wages have barely budged in decades*. Pew research centre 2018.

Dikoetter et al. *Narcotics culture a history of drugs in China*. Hong Kong.University of Chicago press2004

Dammer et al. *Comparing Crime and Justice. In Handbook of Transnational Crime and Justice,* second Edition, Reichel & Albanese. Sage publishing. London 2014 Pages 32-42

Wiland & Bale. *Do no harm, the opioid epidemic* 2018

Dreyer, I & Popescu, N. Brief Issue. European institute for Security. http://www.iss.europa.eu/uploads/media/Brief_11_E urasian_Union.pdf Page 1

Du Pont, R.   *The Selfish Brain: Learning from Addiciton.* American Psychiatric Association. 1997

Edin et al. *The Tenous Attatchments of Working Class Men.* Journal of Economic Perspectives 33 (2) Pages 211-228. 2019

EMCDDA 2015: EMCDDA http://www.emcdda.europa.eu/data/stats2015 & http://www.emcdda.europa.eu/data/stats2015

EMCDDA 2019 CHECK THIS ONE COMES BEFORE THE 2015 ONE

Findlay, M. *The Globalization of Crime: Understanding Transnational Relationships in Context.* Cambridge University Press, Cambridge 2003. Pages 1-20

Flannery, N P. 26 August 2014. 2014 http://latino.foxnews.com/latino/money/2014/05/0 9/cross-border-success-mexican-state-avocado-output-rivals-drug-trade-helps-curb/

Milton Friedman (2009). *"Capitalism and Freedom: Fortieth Anniversary Edition"*, p.14, University of Chicago Press

FT 2008 https://www.rt.com/russia/310571-isis-economy-based-on-illegal/

Fung. J.2018 https://medium.com/@drjasonfung/the-corruption-of-evidence-based-medicine-killing-for-profit-41f2812b8704

Gart.M 2017 https://www.medicaleconomics.com/view/pain-not-fifth-vital-sign

Ghicago Tribune 2019 https://www.chicagotribune.com/business/ct-biz-oxycontin-purdue-pharma-italy-20190529-story.html#:~:text=Dr.%20Guido%20Fanelli%2C%20right%2C%20is%20taken%20to%20the,that%20made%20opioids%20easier%20to%20prescribe%20in%20Italy.

Ghitis, F. *World Citizen: Globalization Fuels the Arab Uprising*. World Politics Review. 10 Feb 2011

Giorgiopoulos, G 2019 https://www.reuters.com/article/us-greece-drugs-idUSKCN1U01IH

Glenny, M. *McMafia*. The Bodley Head, London. 2008 Page 69

Glenny, M. *McMafia*. The Bodley Head, London. 2008 Page 69

Global Health 2017
https://www.ncbi.nlm.nih.gov/pmc/articles/PMC66 34291/#B14

Global   Security   Org.
https://www.globalsecurity.org/intell/world/philippi nes/pnp-corruption.htm

Graham, G. The Daily Telegraph. Drug Laws around the World, Does Anyone Get it Right? 30 October 2014

Graham, G. The Daily Telegraph. Drug Laws around the World, Does Anyone Get it Right? 30 October 2014

Graham, G. The Daily Telegraph. Drug Laws around the World, Does Anyone Get it Right? 30 October 2014

Guardian 2014. 3 October 2014
http://www.theguardian.com/society/2014/oct/03/h eroin-overdose-deaths-us-doubles-painkillers-addiction

Guardian 2013. 25 July 2014.
http://www.theguardian.com/world/2013/jul/25/col ombia-conflict-death-toll-commission

Guardian archive online.
http://www.theguardian.com/theguardian/from-the-archive-blog/2011/jul/22/drugs-trade-richard-nixon

Guardian 2015:
http://www.theguardian.com/world/2015/feb /20/mexico-drugs-trade-el-chapo-arrest-joaquin-guzman-sinaloa-cartel

Guardian 2016   https://www.theguardian.com/us-news/2016/oct/31/opioid-epidemic-dea-official-congress-big-pharma

Guardian Feb 2018
https://www.theguardian.com/world/2018/feb/08/ic c-claims-crimes-against-humanity-duterte-philippines

Guardian Aug 2016.
https://www.theguardian.com/world/2016/a ug/07/rodrigo-duterte-links-150-judges-and-politicians-to-drugs-trade

Guardian 2017.
https://www.theguardian.com/world/2017/nov/12/c arfentanil-bust-canada-fentanyl-opioid-crisis-dangers

Guardian 2014.
http://www.theguardian.com/society/2014/oct/05/-sp-drug-use-is-rising-in-the-uk-but-were-not-addicted

Guardian 2019 https://www.theguardian.com/us-news/2019/may/28/johnson-johnson-opioid-trial-oklahoma

Guardian 2019 https://www.theguardian.com/us-news/2019/jan/24/fda-opioids-big-pharma-prescriptions

Guierrez, E D. The Paradox of Illicit Economic Survival, Resilience, and the Limits of Development and Drug Policy Orthodoxy. Globalisations. Routledge Research Group. 2020.

Hasenclever, A & Weiffen, B. *International Institutions Are the Key: A New Perceptive on the Democratic Peace.* Review of International Studies, Vol 35 issue 4. 2006 Page 563

Hayward & Morrison. *Criminology*, second Edition. Oxford Press. Oxford 2009. Page 84

Hayward & Morrison. *Criminology*, second Edition. Oxford Press. Oxford 2009. Page 81-83

Hayward & Morrison. *Criminology*, second Edition. Oxford Press. Oxford 2009. Page 81

Hayward & Morrison. *Criminology*, second Edition. Oxford Press. Oxford 2009. Page 81

Hayward & Morrison. *Criminology*, second Edition. Oxford Press. Oxford 2009. Page 82-83

Hayward & Morrison. *Criminology*, second Edition. Oxford Press. Oxford 2009. Page 82-83

Hayward & Morrison. *Criminology*, second Edition. Oxford Press. Oxford 2009. Page 82-83

Hayward & Morrison. *Criminology*, second Edition. Oxford Press. Oxford 2009. Page 81

Held et al. *Global Transformations*. Polity press, Cornwall 2000. Pages 9 & 10

Held et al. *Global Transformations*. Polity press, Cornwall 2000. Pages 1-9

Held, D. In Seddon, T. *Drugs, the Informal Economy and Globalization, in the International Journal of Social Economics* Vol 35 (10). Emerald publishing group 2008. Pages 722

Hembra, M. Social, Political and Economic Context of Illegal Drug Abuse in the Philippines. National Institute on Drug Abuse 2004

Hitchens, P. *The War We Never Fought: The British Establishments Surrender to Drugs*. Bloomsbury, London 2012. Page xiii-5

Hitchens, P. *The War We Never Fought: The British Establishments Surrender to Drugs*. Bloomsbury, London 2012. Page 1-5

Horswill, Waylen, Alexander, McKenna. *Do Expert Drivers Have a Reduced Illusion of Superiority?* Transportation Research Parf F: Traffic Psychology and Behaviour 2004. Pages 323-331

Hubbard, B. Worth, R F. Gordon, M R. *Power Vacuum in the Middle East Lifts Militants*. The New York Times. $ Jan 2014

Humphreys et al. Opioids of the Masses, Stopping an American Epidemic From Going Global" Foreign Affairs 2018 https://www.foreignaffairs.com/articles/world/2018-04-16/opioids-masses

Humphreys et al. Opioids of the Masses, Stopping an American Epidemic From Going Global" Foreign Affairs 2018 https://www.foreignaffairs.com/articles/world/2018-04-16/opioids-masses

Humphreys. 2018 Washington Post The government has been undercounting opioid overdose deaths up to 35 percent, study says.https://www.washingtonpost.com/news/wonk/wp/2018/03/12/the-government-has-been-undercounting-opioid-overdose-deaths-up-to-35-percent-study-says/?noredirect=on

Hunter, S, T. *Ideas and Movments Behind the Arab Spring*. Iran Review. 22 August 2015

Husak, D & De Marneffe, P. *The Legalization of the Drugs Debate*. Cambridge 2012. Page 93

Husak, D & De Marneffe, P. *The Legalization of the Drugs Debate*. Cambridge 2012. Page 143

Husak, D & De Marneffe, P. *The Legalization of the Drugs Debate*. Cambridge 2012. Page 195

Husak, D & De Marneffe, P. *The Legalization of the Drugs Debate*. Cambridge 2012. Page 72

Husak, D & De Marneffe, P. *The Legalization of the Drugs Debate*. Cambridge 2012. Pages 75-76

Husak, D & De Marneffe, P. *The Legalization of the Drugs Debate*. Cambridge 2012. Pages 17-24

Husak, D & De Marneffe, P. *The Legalization of the Drugs Debate*. Cambridge 2012. Pages 76

Husak, D & De Marneffe, P. *The Legalization of the Drugs Debate*. Cambridge 2012. Pages 68 & 98

Inciardi, J. *The Drug Legalization Debate*, second edition. Sage publications. Thousand Oaks 1999. Page 23

Inciardi, J. *The Drug Legalization Debate*, second edition. Sage publications. Thousand Oaks 1999. Page 20

Inciardi, J. *The Drug Legalization Debate*, second edition. Sage publications. Thousand Oaks 1999. Page 27

Inciardi, J. *The Drug Legalization Debate*, second edition. Sage publications. Thousand Oaks 1999. Page 56-60

Inciardi, J. *The Drug Legalization Debate*, second edition. Sage publications. Thousand Oaks 1999. Page 37

Inciardi, J. *The Drug Legalization Debate*, second edition. Sage publications. Thousand Oaks 1999. Page 37-38

Inciardi, J. *The Drug Legalization Debate*, second edition. Sage publications. Thousand Oaks 1999. Page 38-40

Inciardi, J. *The Drug Legalization Debate*, second edition. Sage publications. Thousand Oaks 1999. Pages 5-7

Inciardi, J. *The Drug Legalization Debate*, second edition. Sage publications. Thousand Oaks 1999. Pages 80

Inciardi, J. *The Drug Legalization Debate*, second edition. Sage publications. Thousand Oaks 1999. Pages 20-21

Investopedia 2020
https://www.investopedia.com/terms/a/american-dream.asp#:~:text=The%20American%20Dream%20is%20the%20belief%20that%20anyone%2C,risk-taking%2C%20and%20hard%20work%2C%20rather%20than%20by%20chance.

JANIS, IRVING. (1989) *Crucial Decisions: Leadership in Policymaking and Crisis Management.* New York: Free Press.

Jenner, M S. *Handbook of transnational Crime and Justice*: second edition. Reichel & Albanese. Sage London 2014 Page 70

Jenner, M S. *Handbook of transnational Crime and Justice*: second edition. Reichel & Albanese. Sage London 2014. Page 79

Jenner, M S. *Handbook of transnational Crime and Justice*: second edition. Reichel & Albanese. Sage London 2014. Page 79

Jenner, M S. *Handbook of transnational Crime and Justice:* second edition. Reichel & Albanese. Sage London 2014. Page 76-77

Jenner, M S. *Handbook of transnational Crime and Justice*: second edition. Reichel & Albanese. Sage London 2014. Page 76-77

Jenner, M S. *Handbook of transnational Crime and Justice*: second edition. Reichel & Albanese. Sage London 2014. Page 77

Jenner, M S. *Handbook of transnational Crime and Justice*: second edition. Reichel & Albanese. Sage London 2014. Page 82

Jenner, M S. *Handbook of transnational Crime and Justice*: second edition. Reichel & Albanese. Sage London 2014. Page 81

Jenner, M S. *Handbook of transnational Crime and Justice*: second edition. Reichel & Albanese. Sage London 2014. Page 82

Jenner, M S. *Handbook of transnational Crime and Justice*: second edition. Reichel & Albanese. Sage London 2014. Page 65

Jenner, M S. *Handbook of transnational Crime and Justice*: second edition. Reichel & Albanese. Sage London 2014. Page 82

Joutsen, M. *International Instruments on Cooperation in Responding to Transnational Crime. Handbook of transnational Crime and Justice*: second edition. Reichel & Albanese. Sage London 2014. Page 307

Joutsen, M. *International Instruments on Cooperation in Responding to Transnational Crime. Handbook of transnational Crime and Justice*: second edition. Reichel & Albanese. Sage London 2014. Page 308

Joutsen, M. *International Instruments on Cooperation in Responding to Transnational Crime. Handbook of transnational Crime and Justice*: second edition. Reichel & Albanese. Sage London 2014. Page 314

Joutsen, M. *International Instruments on Cooperation in Responding to Transnational Crime. Handbook of transnational Crime and Justice*: second edition. Reichel & Albanese. Sage London 2014. Page 309-310

Kalecki, M. *Political Aspects of Full Employment.* (1943)

Keefer, P & Loayza N. *Innocent Bystanders.* World Bank Publishing, Basingstoke 2010. Page 112

Keefer, P & Loayza N. *Innocent Bystanders.* World Bank Publishing, Basingstoke 2010. Page 114

Keefer, P & Loayza N. World Bank Publishing, *Innocent Bystanders* Basingstoke 2010. Pages 112-113

Keefer, P & Loayza N. *Innocent Bystanders*. World Bank Publishing, Basingstoke 2010. Page 2

Kelly, R J. et al. *Illicit Trafficking: A Reference Handbook*. Santa Barbara 2005. Page 55

Kleiman et al. *Drugs and Drug Policy: What Everyone Needs to Know*. Oxford 2011. Pages 186-187

Kleiman et al. *Drugs and Drug Policy: What Everyone Needs to Know*. Oxford 2011. Page 187

Kleiman et al. *Drugs and Drug Policy: What Everyone Needs to Know*. Oxford 2011. Page 17

Kleiman et al. *Drugs and Drug Policy: What Everyone Needs to Know*. Oxford 2011. Page 53-55

Kleiman et al. *Drugs and Drug Policy: What Everyone Needs to Know*. Oxford 2011. Page 161

Kleiman et al. *Drugs and Drug Policy: What Everyone Needs to Know*. Oxford 2011. Page 166-167

Kleiman et al. *Drugs and Drug Policy: What Everyone Needs to Know*. Oxford 2011. Page 165

Kleiman et al. *Drugs and Drug Policy: What Everyone Needs to Know*. Oxford 2011. Page 165

Kleiman et al. *Drugs and Drug Policy: What Everyone Needs to Know*. Oxford 2011. Page 176

Kleiman et al. *Drugs and Drug Policy: What Everyone Needs to Know*. Oxford 2011. Page 22

Kleiman et al. *Drugs and Drug Policy: What Everyone Needs to Know*. Oxford 2011. Page 19

Kleiman et al. *Drugs and Drug Policy: What Everyone Needs to Know*. Oxford 2011. Page 18, 19&20

Kleiman et al. *Drugs and Drug Policy: What Everyone Needs to Know*. Oxford 2011. Page 76

Kleiman et al. *Drugs and Drug Policy: What Everyone Needs to Know*. Oxford 2011. Page 165

Kleiman et al. *Drugs and Drug Policy: What Everyone Needs to Know*. Oxford 2011. Page 167

Kleiman et al. *Drugs and Drug Policy: What Everyone Needs to Know*. Oxford 2011. Page 165

Klerks, P. *Transnational Organized Crime: Perspectives on Global Security*. Routledge, London 2003. Pages 99 & 100

Klerks, P. *Transnational Organized Crime: Perspectives on Global Security*. Routledge, London 2003. Pages 99 & 100

Klerman, Gerlad L. *Psychotropic Hedonism Vs Pharmacological Calvanism*. The Hastings Centre Report Vol 2 Nr 4 (1972)

Klerman, Gerlad L. *Psychotropic Hedonism Vs Pharmacological Calvanism*. The Hastings Centre Report Vol 2 Nr 4 (1972) Page 3

Kuznetsova, R. *Crime in Russia: Causes and Preventions*. Demokratziya 2,3. 1995.Pages 442-452

Lamy, S L. *In The Globalization of World Politics* :An Introduction to International Relations, Baylis et al. Oxford 2011 Page 121-122

Lankow, A. *The Real North Korea: Life Politics in the Failed Stalinist Utopia*. Oxford 2015. Page 268

Lankow, A. *The Real North Korea: Life Politics in the Failed Stalinist Utopia*. Oxford 2015. Page 22-23

Lankow, A. *The Real North Korea: Life Politics in the Failed Stalinist Utopia*. Oxford 2015. Page 88-89

Lasco, G. 2018 https://theconversation.com/just-how-big-is-the-drug-problem-in-the-philippines-anyway-66640

LA Time, 2016 https://www.latimes.com/projects/la-me-oxycontin-part3/#:~:text=OxyContin%20goes%20global%20%E2%80%94%20%E2%80%9CWe%E2%80%99re%20only%20just%20getting,began%20to%20fall%20in%20the%20U.S.%20in%202011.

Levi, M. *Money Laundering and its Regulation* .Annals of the American Academy of Political and Social Science 2002. Page 191

Linklater, A. *The Globalization of World Politics*: An Introduction to International Relations, Baylis et al. Oxford 2011 Page 532

MacCoun et al. *:* in Journal of drug issues, 23(4) 615-629

Mansfield and Fishstein. *Eyes still wide shut: Counternarcotics in Transition in Afghanistan. Christian Aid Study on Drugs and Illicit Practices* 2015 pp. 5–8

Martin, C A. *Terrorism and Transnational Organized Crime. In the Handbook or Transnational Crime and Justice,* second Edition. Sage, London. 2014. Page 247

Martin, C A. *Terrorism and Transnational Organized Crime. In the Handbook or Transnational Crime and Justice,* second Edition. Sage, London. 2014. Page 247-249

Martin, C A. *Terrorism and Transnational Organized Crime. In the Handbook or Transnational Crime and Justice,* second Edition. Sage, London. 2014. Page 251-259

Martin, C A. *Terrorism and Transnational Organized Crime. In the Handbook or Transnational Crime and Justice,* second Edition. Sage, London. 2014. Page 75

Martin, C A. *Terrorism and Transnational Organized Crime. In the Handbook or Transnational*

Crime and Justice, second Edition. Sage, London. 2014. Page 252

Martin, C A. *Terrorism and Transnational Organized Crime. In the Handbook or Transnational Crime and Justice*, second Edition. Sage, London. 2014. Page 260

Mausfeld, R. *Why are the lambs silent?* Westend, Frankfurt a.M. 2019. Page 101

McCoy, A W. *The Politics of Heroin: CIA Complicity in the Global Drug trade*, revised edition. Lawrence Hill Books. Chicago 2003

McCoy, A W. *The Politics of Heroin: CIA Complicity in the Global Drug trade*, revised edition. Lawrence Hill Books. Chicago 2003 Pages xxi-xxii

McCoy, A W. *The Politics of Heroin: CIA Complicity in the Global Drug trade*, revised edition. Lawrence Hill Books. Chicago 2003 Pages 19, 443-444, 445, 449

McGrew, A. in *The globalization of world politics*: an introduction to international relations. Baylis et al. 24-26 Oxford Publishers, Oxford 2011. Pages

Mills, J S. *On Liberty and other writings.* 1869 reprinted by Cambridge, 1989. Page 57

Mills, J S. *On Liberty and other writings.* 1869 reprinted by Cambridge, 1989. Page 62

Mills, J S. *On Liberty and other writings.* 1869 reprinted by Cambridge, 1989. Page 56

Misailidi, N et al. Fentanyls continue to replace heroin in the drug arena: the case of ocfentanil and carfentanil. 2017

Monbiot. G. *Neoliberalism - the ideology at the root of all our problems*. Guardian 15th April 2016

Morrison, K. *Marx Durkheim Weber, Formations of Modern Social Thought*. Sage, London. Page 124-125

Mulrooney 2015
https://law.marquette.edu/assets/news-and-events/pdf/marquette-law-review-mulrooney-legel.pdf

Murphy. R (2017)
https://www.taxresearch.org.uk/Blog/2017/07/25/there-is-no-laffer-effect-in-uk-corporation-tax/

Musto, F. *The American Disease: The Origins of Narcotics Control*. Oxford Press 1999.Page 61

Musto, F. *The American Disease: The Origins of Narcotics Control*. Oxford Press 1999. Pages 51-68

Musto, F. *The American Disease: The Origins of Narcotics Control*. Oxford Press 1999. Page 65-66

Musto, F. *The American Disease: The Origins of Narcotics Control*. Oxford Press 1999. Page 24-53

Naim, M. *Illicit*. First Anchor books, New York. 2005. Pages 17-18

Naim, M. *Illicit*. First Anchor books, New York. 2005. Pages 5-6

Naim, M. in *Globalization and Crime*. Aas, K F. Sage publications, London 2007. Page 102

Naim, M. *Illicit*. First Anchor books, New York. 2005. Page 4

Naim, M. *Illicit*. First Anchor books, New York. 2005. Page 4

Naim, M. *Illicit*. First Anchor books, New York. 2005. Pages 81-85

Naim, M. *Illicit*. First Anchor books, New York. 2005. Pages 263

Naim, M. *Illicit*. First Anchor books, New York. 2005. Pages 242

Naim, M. *Illicit*. First Anchor books, New York. 2005. Pages 256-259

Naim, M. *Illicit*. First Anchor books, New York. 2005. Pages 265

Naim, M. *Illicit*. First Anchor books, New York. 2005. Pages 256

Naim, M. *Illicit*. First Anchor books, New York. 2005. Pages 192

Naim, M. *Illicit*. First Anchor books, New York. 2005. Pages 183

Naim, M. *Illicit.* First Anchor books, New York. 2005. Pages 175-198

Naim, M. *Illicit.* First Anchor books, New York. 2005. Pages 80

Naim, M. *Illicit.* First Anchor books, New York. 2005. Pages 68

Naim, M. *Illicit.* First Anchor books, New York. 2005. Pages 180

Naim, M. *In Transnational Crime and Justice*, second edition. Ed Peichel, P & Albanese, J. Sage publications, London 2014. Page notes 82

Naim, M. In *Transnational Crime and Justice*, second edition. Ed Peichel, P & Albanese, J. Sage publications, London 2014. Page notes 89

Naim, M. In *Transnational Crime and Justice*, second edition. Ed Peichel, P & Albanese, J. Sage publications, London 2014. Page notes 261-265

Naim, M. In *Transnational Crime and Justice*, second edition. Ed Peichel, P & Albanese, J. Sage publications, London 2014. Page notes 28-29

Newman, R K. *Opium Smoking in Late Imperial China*". Modern Asia Studies 29.Pages 765-794

Newman, R K. *Opium Smoking in Late Imperial China*". Modern Asia Studies 29.Pages 765-794

Nicol, D. *The Constitutional protection of capitalism.* Hart Publishing Oxford 2010. Pages 3-5

Nutt, D. *Drugs without the Hot Air.* UIT Cambridge, Cambridge 2012. Page 189

Nutt, D. *Drugs without the Hot Air.* UIT Cambridge, Cambridge 2012. Page 161-162

Nutt, D. *Drugs without the Hot Air.* UIT Cambridge, Cambridge 2012. Page 161-162

Nutt, D. *Drugs without the Hot Air.* UIT Cambridge, Cambridge 2012. Page 162

Nutt, D. Guardian Tuesday 19th June 2012

Nutt, D. Guardian Tuesday 19th June 2012

Nutt, D. Guardian Tuesday 19th June 2012

Nutt, D. Guardian Thursday 29 Oct 2009. http://www.theguardian.com/politics/2009/oct/29/nutt-drugs-policy-reform-call

Obaji, P. https://www.thedailybeast.com/inside-the-networks-of-sex-slaves-the-drug-trade-colombian-cartels-and-al-qaeda-in-africa **2018**

O'Donnell, C. *New Study Quantifies Use of Social Media in Arab Spring.* University of Washington 12 September 2011

Passas, G. *Global Anomie, Dysnomie and Economic Crime*: Hidden Consequences of Neolibrealism and

Globalization in Russia and Around the World. Social Justice 27.2. Pages 19

Passas, G. *Global Anomie, Dysnomie and Economic Crime*: Hidden Consequences of Neolibrealism and Globalization in Russia and Around the World. Social Justice 27.2. Pages 19-21

Passas, G. *Global Anomie, Dysnomie and Economic Crime: Hidden Consequences of Neolibrealism and Globalization in Russia and Around the World.* Social Justice 27.2. Pages 29-31

Passas, G. *Global Anomie, Dysnomie and Economic Crime: Hidden Consequences of Neolibrealism and Globalization in Russia and Around the World.* Social Justice 27.2. Pages 29-31

Passas, G. *Global Anomie, Dysnomie and Economic Crime: Hidden Consequences of Neolibrealism and Globalization in Russia and Around the World.* Social Justice 27.2. Pages 29-31

Passas, G. *Global Anomie, Dysnomie and Economic Crime: Hidden Consequences of Neolibrealism and Globalization in Russia and Around the World.* Social Justice 27.2. Pages 35

Passas, G. *Global Anomie, Dysnomie and Economic Crime: Hidden Consequences of Neolibrealism and Globalization in Russia and Around the World.* Social Justice 27.2. Pages 35

Passas, G. *Global Anomie, Dysnomie and Economic Crime: Hidden Consequences of Neolibrealism and Globalization in Russia and Around the World.* Social Justice 27.2. Pages 38-41

Passas, G. *Global Anomie, Dysnomie and Economic Crime: Hidden Consequences of Neolibrealism and Globalization in Russia and Around the World.* Social Justice 27.2. Pages 38-39

Passas, G. *Global Anomie, Dysnomie and Economic Crime: Hidden Consequences of Neolibrealism and Globalization in Russia and Around the World.* Social Justice 27.2. Pages 38-39

Paoli et al. *The Development of an Illegal Market: Drug Consumption and Trade in Post-Soviet Russia.* 2002. British Journal of Criminology 42, 21-39. Pages 22 & 24

Paoli et al. *The World Heroin Market.* Oxford University Press 2009. Page 19

Paoli et al. *The World Heroin Market.* Oxford University Press 2009. Page 19

Paoli et al. *The World Heroin Market.* Oxford University Press 2009. Page 185&186

Paoli et al. *The World Heroin Market.* Oxford University Press 2009. Page 181

Paoli et al. *The World Heroin Market.* Oxford University Press 2009. Page186

Paoli et al. *The World Heroin Market*. Oxford University Press 2009. Pages 5-7

Paoli et al. *The World Heroin Market*. Oxford University Press 2009. Page 119

Paoli et al. *The World Heroin Market*. Oxford University Press 2009. Page 17

Paoli et al. *The World Heroin Market*. Oxford University Press 2009. Page 210

Pearson, G & Patel, K. *Drugs and Deprivation and Ethnicity: Outreach among Asian drug users in a Northern English city*. Journal of drug issues. Vol 28/1. Pages 199-224

Petersen, J. 2018. https://www.youtube.com/watch?v=sZH0N9aECa0

Powell, in *The Global Complexities of September 11th, Theory, Culture & Society*. Urry, J. Pages 57-69

PresidentsCommission(2017) https://www.whitehouse.gov/sites/whitehouse.gov/files/images/Final_Report_Draft_11-1-2017.pdf

Pridmore, A& Kim, S W. *Democratization and Political Change as Threats to the Collective Sentiment, Testing Durkheim in Russia*. The Annals of American Academy of Political and Social Science Vol 605. Pages 82-83

Prodi,R.2020.https://www.ilmessaggero.it/editoriali/romano_prodi/coronavirus_europa-5137245.html

Ranstorp, M. *Microfinancing the Caliphate: how the Islamic State is Unlocking the Assets of European Recruits.* 2016

Redo & Platzer. In the *Handbook of transnational Crime and Justice*: second edition. Reichel & Albanese. Sage London 2014 Page 288

Reuters Dec 2017 https://www.reuters.com/article/us-philippines-drugs-idUSKBN1YO184

Reuters Apr 2018. https://uk.reuters.com/article/uk-philippines-duterte-police-special-re/special-report-police-describe-kill-rewards-staged-crime-scenes-in-dutertes-drug-war-idUKKBN17K1EB

Reuters. 2020. https://www.reuters.com/article/legal-us-purdue-pharma-investigation-opi-idUSKBN1ZR2T8

Reuters Jan 2020 https://www.reuters.com/article/us-philippines-drugs-idUSKBN1ZD21Q

Rittberger, V & Zangl, B. *International Organizations: Polity, Politics and Policies* .Palgrave MacMillian. London 2006. Page 15

Rolling Stone 2018 https://www.rollingstone.com/culture/culture-news/opioid-fda-dsuvia-sufentanil-approved-752252/

RT 2013 https://www.rt.com/usa/311023-congress-heroin-epidemic-source/

RT 2015 https://www.rt.com/russia/310571-isis-economy-based-on-illegal/

Salavitz,M.2016 https://www.washingtonpost.com/posteverything/wp/2016/10/06/why-we-ignore-thousands-of-killings-in-the-philippines-the-victims-were-drug-users/

Sarpatwari, A et al. The Opioid Epidemic: Fixing a Broken Pharmaceutical Market. Harvard Press 2017. Page 463

Sarpatwari, A et al. The Opioid Epidemic: Fixing a Broken Pharmaceutical Market. Harvard Press 2017. Page 472 & 473

Schoff, E N et al. Qualitative Identification of Fentanyl Analogs and Other Opioids in Postmortem Cases by UHPLC-Ion Trap-MSn 2017

Schottenfeld, J. 5 May 2015 Foreign Affairs. https://www.foreignaffairs.com/articles/tajikistan/2015-05-11/tajikistans-russian-dream

Seddon, T. *Drugs, the Informal Economy and Globalization, in the International Journal of Social Economics* Vol 35 (10). Emerald publishing group 2008. Pages 721-724

Seddon, T. *Drugs, the Informal Economy and Globalization, in the International Journal of Social Economics* Vol 35 (10). Emerald publishing group 2008. Pages 721-722

Seddon, T. *Drugs, the Informal Economy and Globalization, in the International Journal of Social Economics* Vol 35 (10). Emerald publishing group 2008. Pages 722

Seddon, T. *Drugs, the Informal Economy and Globalization, in the International Journal of Social Economics* Vol 35 (10). Emerald publishing group 2008. Pages 723

Seddon, T. *Drugs, the Informal Economy and Globalization, in the International Journal of Social Economics* Vol 35 (10). Emerald publishing group 2008. Pages 724

Sheptycki, J. *In Transnational Organized Crime: Perspectives on Global Security*. Ed Edwards, A& Gill, P. Routledge, Abindon, Oxon 2003. Pages 42-55

Sheptycki, J. *In Transnational Organized Crime: Perspectives on Global Security*. Ed Edwards, A& Gill, P. Routledge, Abindon, Oxon 2003. Pages 43-46, 51, 52, 54 & 55

Sheptycki, J. *In Transnational Organized Crime: Perspectives on Global Security*. Ed Edwards, A& Gill, P. Routledge, Abindon, Oxon 2003. Pages 42-55

Sheptycki, J. *Law Enforcment, Justice and Democracy in the Transnational Arena: Reflections on the War on Drugs*. International Journal of the Sociology of Law. 1996. Edinburgh. Pages 70-72

Sheptycki, J. *Law Enforcment, Justice and Democracy in the Transnational Arena: Reflections on the War on Drugs*. International Journal of the Sociology of Law. 1996. Edinburgh. Page 65

Shiptechnology.com http://www.ship-technology.com/features/feature-the-worlds-10-biggest-ports/

Siegel, L J. Criminology 9th edition. University of Massachusetts. 2006. 254-271

Slobodian, Q. *Globalists, The End of Empire and the Birth of Neoliberalism*. Harvard. 2018 pages 1-26

Smeulers & Hoax. *Studying the Microdynamics of the Rwandan Genocide.* British Jorurnal of Criminology. 2010

Stares, P B. *Global Habit: The Drug Problem in a Borderless world*. Brookings Institution, Washington 1996. Pages 18

Stares, P B. *Global Habit: The Drug Problem in a Borderless world*. Brookings Institution, Washington 1996. Pages 63&64

Stares, P B. *Global Habit: The Drug Problem in a Borderless world*. Brookings Institution, Washington 1996. Page 66

Stares, P B. *Global Habit: The Drug Problem in a Borderless world*. Brookings Institution, Washington 1996. Pages 66&67

Stares, P B. *Global Habit: The Drug Problem in a Borderless world*. Brookings Institution, Washington 1996. Pages 66&67

Stares, P B. *Global Habit: The Drug Problem in a Borderless world*. Brookings Institution, Washington 1996. Pages 64

Stares, P B. *Global Habit: The Drug Problem in a Borderless world*. Brookings Institution, Washington 1996. Pages 71

Stares, P B. *Global Habit: The Drug Problem in a Borderless world*. Brookings Institution, Washington 1996. Pages 5

Stares, P B. *Global Habit: The Drug Problem in a Borderless world*. Brookings Institution, Washington 1996. Page 68

Stares, P B. *Global Habit: The Drug Problem in a Borderless world*. Brookings Institution, Washington 1996. Page 69

Stares, P B. *Global Habit: The Drug Problem in a Borderless world*. Brookings Institution, Washington 1996. Page 74&92

Stares, P B. *Global Habit: The Drug Problem in a Borderless world*. Brookings Institution, Washington 1996. Page 65

Stares, P B. *Global Habit: The Drug Problem in a Borderless world*. Brookings Institution, Washington 1996. Page 64

Stares, P B. *Global Habit: The Drug Problem in a Borderless world.* Brookings Institution, Washington 1996. Page 99

Stares, P B. *Global Habit: The Drug Problem in a Borderless world.* Brookings Institution, Washington 1996. Pages 86, 87, 102, 103

Stares, P B. *Global Habit: The Drug Problem in a Borderless world.* Brookings Institution, Washington 1996. Pages 86, 87, 102, 103

Stiglitz, J. *The Euro and its Threat to the Future of Europe.* Penguin. St Ives UK. 2017. Page 131-132

Streeck, W. Buying Time, The Delayed Crisis of Democratic Capitalism 2nd edition. Verso. London 2017. Page xxvi

Swanson, E. http://www.huffingtonpost.com/2013/12/18/drug-sentencing_n_4461634.html

Taylor, I. *The New European Criminology: Crime and Social Order in Europe.* Ed Ruggiero, V et al. Routledge 1998. Page 32

Thomas, C. *The Constitution of Equality: Democratic Authority and its Limits.* Oxford 2008. Pages 1-8

Thomas Reuters 2020 https://uk.practicallaw.thomsonreuters.com/0-624-6147?contextData=(sc.Default)&transitionType=Default&firstPage=true&bhcp=1

Thornton, M. CATO Institute policy analysis: *Prohibition was a failure*. 1991. Page 2

Thornton, M. CATO Institute policy analysis: *Prohibition was a failure*. 1991. Page 8

Thornton, M. CATO Institute policy analysis: *Prohibition was a failure*. 1991. Page 2

Tombs, S. in *Criminology*, second edition. Oxford, Oxford 2009. Page 307

Tombs, S. in *Criminology*, second edition. Oxford, Oxford 2009. Page 307

Townsend, M. Guardian 5 October 2014. Huge majority things war on drugs has failed, new poll finds.

Tooze. A. *Der Tod des Mythos Zentralbank*. Heinrich Boell Stiftung. 2020

Tuck, R. *Natural Rights Theories, their Origin and their Development*. Cambridge University Press. Cambridge. 1979

Tuckman J. The Guardian 4 May 2015. http://www.theguardian.com/world/2015/may/04/mexico-declares-war-rising-drug-cartel-downs-military-helicopter

Tuckman, J. The Guardian 20 Febuary 2015. http://www.theguardian.com/world/2015/feb/20/mexico-drugs-trade-el-chapo-arrest-joaquin-guzman-sinaloa-cartel

UK Parliament.
http://www.publications.parliament.uk/pa/cm200910/cmselect/cmhaff/74/7410.htm

UNODC https://www.unodc.org/unodc/treaties/

UNODC
2008https://www.unodc.org/documents/data-and-analysis/Studies/100_Years_of_Drug_Control.pdf
Page 3

UNODC 2015
https://www.unodc.org/documents/wdr2015/World_Drug_Report_2015.pdf Page 11

UNODC 2015
https://www.unodc.org/documents/wdr2015/World_Drug_Report_2015.pdf   Page 11

UNODC 2010. *The Globalization of Crime: A Transnational Crime Threat Assessment.* United Nations Publications 2010. Page 76

UNODC 2003. *The Opium Economy in Afghanistan: An International Problem.* UN Press. Page 68

UNODC Online:
http://www.unodc.org/unodc/treaties/

UNODC 2009.
https://www.unodc.org/unodc/en/frontpage/2009/December/security-council-debates-devastating-impact-of-drug-trafficking.html

UNODC 2015 World Drug Report.
https://www.unodc.org/documents/wdr2015/World
_Drug_Report_2015.pdf

UNODC 2015 World Drug Report.
https://www.unodc.org/documents/wdr2015/World
_Drug_Report_2015.pdf

UNODC 2017 World Drug Report

UNODC 2018 World Drugs Report UNODC, 2018a,
pp. 1 and 8

UNODC 2019 World Drug Report

UNODC 2019 World Drug Report page 52

UNODC IRI 2016
*https://www.unodc.org/islamicrepublicofiran/en/th
e-international-drug-control-treaties-do-not-
mandate-a-war-on-drugs-says-incb-report.html*

UN 1988.
http://www.unodc.org/documents/commissions/CN
D/Int_Drug_Control_Conventions/Ebook/The_Inter
national_Drug_Control_Conventions_E.pdf Page 127

UN 1988.
http://www.unodc.org/documents/commissions/CN
D/Int_Drug_Control_Conventions/Ebook/The_Inter
national_Drug_Control_Conventions_E.pdf Page
132-141

UN 1988.
http://www.unodc.org/documents/commissions/CN

D/Int_Drug_Control_Conventions/Ebook/The_Inter
national_Drug_Control_Conventions_E.pdf Page 127

United nations 1998.
http://www.un.org/press/en/1998/19980609.ga9416.h
tml

US Deprt State ***https://www.state.gov/bureau-
of-international-narcotics-and-law-
enforcement-affairs-philippines-summary/***

Van Creveld, M. *The Transformation of War*. New
York Free Press. Page 5-6

Van Duyne & Levi. *Drugs and Money: Managing the
Drug Trade and Crime-Money in Europe*. Routledge
2006. Page 14

Van Duyne & Levi. *Drugs and Money: Managing the
Drug Trade and Crime-Money in Europe*. Routledge
2006. Page 19-24

Van Duyne & Levi. Drugs and Money: Managing the
Drug Trade and Crime-Money in Europe. Routledge
2006. Page 5

Van Duyne & Levi. *Drugs and Money: Managing the
Drug Trade and Crime-Money in Europe*. Routledge
2006. Page 13,14&26

Van Duyne & Levi. *Drugs and Money: Managing the Drug Trade and Crime-Money in Europe.* Routledge 2006. Page 9

Van Duyne & Levi. *Drugs and Money: Managing the Drug Trade and Crime-Money in Europe.* Routledge 2006. Page

Van Duyne & Levi. *Drugs and Money: Managing the Drug Trade and Crime-Money in Europe.* Routledge 2006. Page 19-24

Van Duyne & Levi. *Drugs and Money: Managing the Drug Trade and Crime-Money in Europe.* Routledge 2006. Page 24

Van Duyne & Levi. *Drugs and Money: Managing the Drug Trade and Crime-Money in Europe.* Routledge 2006. Page 44, 48&49

Van Duyne & Levi. *Drugs and Money: Managing the Drug Trade and Crime-Money in Europe.* Routledge 2006. Page 76

Van Duyne & Levi. *Drugs and Money: Managing the Drug Trade and Crime-Money in Europe.* Routledge 2006. Page 1-18

Van Duyne & Levi. *Drugs and Money: Managing the Drug Trade and Crime-Money in Europe.* Routledge 2006. Page 1-18

Vargas, J E. *Arab Awakening: How an Egyptian Revolution Began on Facebook. New York Times* February 17 2012

Vulliamy, E. The Guardian 24 July 2011.
http://www.theguardian.com/society/2011/jul/24/war-on-drugs-40-years

Washington Post 2011
https://www.washingtonpost.com/blogs/plum-line/post/theres-been-class-warfare-for-the-last-20-years-and-my-class-has-won/2011/03/03/gIQApaFbAL_blog.html

Washington Post 2016
https://www.washingtonpost.com/investigations/key-officials-switch-sides-from-dea-to-pharmaceutical-industry/2016/12/22/55d2e938-c07b-11e6-b527-949c5893595e_story.html

Washington Post 2019
https://www.washingtonpost.com/

WHO   2015
http://www.who.int/tobacco/mpower/tobacco_facts/en/

WHO   2015
http://www.who.int/substance_abuse/facts/alcohol/en/

Wincup & Tranor. Drugs, Alcohol and Crime. In *Criminology* second edition. Oxford 2009. Pagess234-235

Williams,   M.
http://theconflictarchives.com/news/2019/5/15/libya-trafficking 2019

Wilson, W. *Criminal Law: Doctrine and theory*, third edition. Pearson Education Limited. Harlow 2008. Pages 58 & 59

Woodwiss, M. In *Transnational Organized Crime: Perspectives on Global Security*. Ed Edwards, A& Gill, P. Routledge, Abindon, Oxon 2003. Pages 19

Woodwiss, M. In *Transnational Organized Crime: Perspectives on Global Security*. Ed Edwards, A& Gill, P. Routledge, Abindon, Oxon 2003. Pages 17-22

Woodwiss, M. In *Transnational Organized Crime: Perspectives on Global Security*. Ed Edwards, A& Gill, P. Routledge, Abindon, Oxon 2003. Pages 20 & 24

Zibbell, J E. Association of Law Enforcement Seizures of Heroin, Fentanyl, and Carfentanil With Opioid Overdose Deaths in Ohio, 2014-2017. 2020 JAMA network

I WOULD ALSO LIKE TO SAY A SPECIAL THANKS TO EDINA BRECHLER FOR ALL HER SUPPORT. TO MY SISTER KIM. TO MY BROTHER PETER WHO IS AFFLICTED BY A LOVE FOR LFC AND TO TOPSY THE WORLDS MOST UNSOCIABLE CAT. AND TO MY FATHER IN GERMANY. AND TO MR DI LORENZO FOR ENCOURAGING ME TO WRITE.